John Calvin Rediscovered

Princeton Theological Seminary Studies in Reformed Theology and History

John Calvin Rediscovered

The Impact of His Social and Economic Thought

EDWARD DOMMEN AND
JAMES D. BRATT, EDITORS

Princeton Theological Seminary Studies in Reformed Theology and History

Westminster John Knox Press
LOUISVILLE • LONDON

Book design by Sharon Adams
Cover design by Jennifer K. Cox

First edition
Published by Westminster John Knox Press
Louisville, Kentucky

This book is printed on acid-free paper that meets the American National Standards Institute Z39.48 standard. ♾

PRINTED IN THE UNITED STATES OF AMERICA

07 08 09 10 11 12 13 14 15 16 — 10 9 8 7 6 5 4 3 2

Library of Congress Cataloging-in-Publication Data

John Calvin rediscovered : the impact of his social and economic thought / Edward Dommen and James D. Bratt, editors.
p. cm. — (Princeton Theological Seminary studies in reformed theology and history)
Includes bibliographical references and index.
ISBN 978-0-664-23227-6 (alk. paper)
1. Calvin, Jean, 1509–1564. 2. Calvin, Jean, 1509–1564—Influence. 3. Christian Sociology. 4. Church and social problems. I. Dommen, Edward. II. Bratt, James D., 1949–
BX9418.J63 2007
261.8092—dc22 2007011289

Contents

Introduction

EDWARD DOMMEN

John Calvin lived entirely in an urban environment and was bathed in the atmosphere of nascent capitalism. His parents were bourgeois of Noyon in northern France, where his father was an ecclesiastical administrator. John's early studies were not in theology but in law and letters. When he found it prudent to leave France in early 1535, he went to Basel, a great trading center. When passing through Geneva in mid-1536, at the age of 27, he was induced to stay and organize the Reformed church there. Geneva also was a long-established center of trade and finance as well as manufacturing. When he was forced to leave in 1538, he settled in yet another trading city, Strasbourg, before returning in 1541 to Geneva, where he remained until his death in 1564. In this setting, his everyday contacts called upon him to deal with the moral problems of an urban economy. As a result, he thought more deeply about the subject than the other leading reformers of his time. For instance, he set out his arguments concerning the legitimacy of interest—a key opening the door to the modern economy—in a letter replying to an inquiry the banker Claude de Sachin had addressed to him.[1] There are those who say that Calvin was the father of capitalism. Whether or not one wishes to go that far, there is no denying that he was present at the birth.

Calvin's economic and social teaching was so thoroughly absorbed into the cultural subconscious of Latin Protestants that its particular source was

1. Edward Dommen, "Calvin et le prêt à intérêt," *Finance & bien commun* 16 (Autumn 2003): 42–58.

generally forgotten. In the Anglo-Saxon world, it was largely swamped within a century or so by Puritanism, a very different system. When Ernst Troeltsch and above all Max Weber were arguing the intimate relationship between Protestantism and capitalism, it was basically Puritanism that they took as their reference.[2] In this regard, Christoph Stückelberger quotes in his essay in this volume an explicit footnote of Weber's: "I may here say definitely that we are not studying the personal views of Calvin, but Calvinism, and that in the form to which it had evolved by the end of the sixteenth and in the seventeenth centuries in the great areas where it had a decisive influence and which were at the same time the home of capitalistic culture."[3]

Weber and Troeltsch were writing before the rediscovery of Calvin's own teachings, which Edmond Perret dates back only to the 1930s.[4] After that the word "Calvinian," which had likewise been forgotten, reappeared in the vocabulary.[5] "Calvinian" refers to Calvin's own teaching and its spirit, as distinct from "Calvinist," which refers to the theology of the Reformed churches and those who follow the teaching of those churches as it has changed with time and place.[6] Edmond Perret illustrates the distinction in terms of the slogan *ecclesia reformata semper reformanda*. As he puts it, "Calvinist" refers to the Reformed churches as institutions (*reformata*), while "Calvinian" refers to Calvin as a touchstone in the unending process of reformation (*reformanda*).

A high point in the rediscovery of Calvin was the publication in 1961 of André Biéler's *La pensée économique et sociale de Calvin*. This monumental work consists of a meticulous compilation of quotations from Calvin's own writings on economic and social issues, inserted into a masterful commentary. Until 1990, however, when it was translated into Portuguese, it remained accessible only to people capable of reading French. Eduardo Galasso's essay describes the context of this event.

The book has at last been translated into English.[7] In order to mark its publication, the World Alliance of Reformed Churches, the University of Geneva Faculty of Theology, and the John Knox International Reformed Center held an international consultation on "The Impact of Calvin's Economic and Social

2. Ernst Troeltsch, "Die Soziallehren der christlichen Kirchen und Gruppen," in *Gesammelte Schriften I* (Tübingen, 1912). ET: *The Social Teaching of the Christian Churches* (New York: George Allen & Unwin, 1931); Max Weber, "Die protestantische Ethik und der Geist des Kapitalismus," in *Archiv für Sozialwissenschaft und Sozialpolitik* (Tübingen, 1904–1905). ET: *The Protestant Ethic and the Spirit of Capitalism* (1930).

3. Weber, *Protestant Ethic*, 220n7.

4. Perret is a former secretary-general of the World Alliance of Reformed Churches. He shared this with me in a personal communication.

5. It was originally invented in 1560 by the French poet Ronsard (*Le Grand Robert*).

6. See Seong-Won Park's essay in this volume.

7. *Calvin's Economic and Social Thought* (Geneva: World Council of Churches, 2005).

Thought on Reformed Witness" in Geneva on November 3–6, 2004. This book assembles several of the contributions to the consultation. Others were published in the December 2005 issue of *Reformed World*.

The collection in this volume is divided into three parts. The first presents a set of insights into Calvin's own economic, social, and environmental thought. The second describes the rediscovery of Calvin in different times and places, starting with precursors in the late nineteenth and early twentieth centuries. It then moves on to describe the splash that was created by Calvin's own ideas landing in the Protestant pond that missionaries, mostly from the United States, had earlier dug in countries in Latin America and Asia. The third section deals with the pitfalls of translating Calvin's ideas faithfully from one language to another, or from the language of one period into that of another, against the treacherous background of the unstated presuppositions of each.

The preparation and publication of this volume were aided by a timely grant from the Center for Christian Scholarship at Calvin College in Grand Rapids, Michigan. The Center joins the authors and editors in hoping that this volume will encourage deeper exploration into what Calvin's economic and social teaching has to say to the world today.

PART 1

Calvin and His Age

1

The Character and Significance of John Calvin's Teaching on Social and Economic Issues

Elsie Anne McKee

To grasp John Calvin's teaching on social and economic matters, it is helpful to set it in the context of his wider biblical and practical theology, which shapes and conditions all his other teachings. When that is done, it is evident how social and economic themes are interwoven with the fundamental character of Calvin's theology, and it is also possible to point out practical applications of his teaching and to assess the significance of his ideas for the sixteenth century and later.

CALVIN'S BIBLICAL AND PRACTICAL THEOLOGY

Calvin's Religious Purpose and Audience

The central focus of Calvin's work was to instruct and exhort Christians in the purpose for which they were created, that is, to know and love and serve the triune God, Father, Son, and Holy Spirit, who creates, redeems, and gives faith. This purpose is also the greatest human good, the fulfillment and meaning of human life.[1] The existential entry point into this knowledge of God is effected by the Holy Spirit through faith, making the person chosen by God

1. "The Catechism of the Church of Geneva," in *Calvin: Theological Treatises*, ed. J. K. S. Reid (Philadelphia: Westminster, 1954), 91.

know and trust God's goodwill in Christ for himself or herself.[2] Calvin assumes that he is addressing believers, people who confess Jesus Christ as their only Savior. Because they know the Redeemer, believers also know their Creator. Because the God they know through the work of the Holy Spirit is the One who loved them enough to die for their sins and grant them full acceptance purely by divine grace, believers also know that this God is constantly watching over them in this life and preparing them for a place in the life to come.

In addition to the salvific work of Christ, the Creator has endowed the world and especially human beings with many amazing earthly gifts so that nothing may be lacking for good in all creation.[3] Because of human sin, however, that creation is no longer perfect as God made it, but God's goodness still shines in the universe for those who have the eyes of faith and spectacles of Scripture to discern it (1.6.1). To make sense of Calvin's teaching, it is essential to recognize that what he says about social and economic life is rooted in his understanding of God as Creator but is also conditioned by the fact that he is addressing people who know God the Redeemer. Even though believers share socioeconomic dimensions of life with nonbelievers, what Calvin says about these earthly matters is determined by his understanding of the work of the Holy Spirit in Christians.

Axioms, Presuppositions, and the Knowledge of God

Calvin operates with certain axioms, assumptions about truth that require no proof. (This is true for all people, whether they recognize it or not.) One of Calvin's axioms is the conviction that God is good and just and that what God wills is good and right by definition. No evidence is necessary, but explanations may be given so that what is believed may be understood and practiced. Another axiom is that Christ is the sole Savior and that no one can rightly know God without coming to God through Christ. A third axiom is that the Bible is the sole and sufficient revelation of God's will; nothing can be added or ignored, and no speculation may fill in what look to us like gaps. More significantly, this revelation is unified because God is the one original Author. Calvin readily recognizes the roles of the human authors of Scripture and the differences among them, but it is axiomatic for him that all that people need to know for salvation is in the Bible. Moreover, all that they need to practice will be coherently practicable when it is rightly understood.

2. Calvin, *Institutes of the Christian Religion* 3.2.7; ed. John T. McNeill, trans. Ford Lewis Battles, LCC (Philadelphia: Westminster, 1960). In some cases where I have quoted from the edition, I have made minor alterations to make the text more easily readable. Subsequent citations are given in the text.

3. Calvin, *Commentaries on the First Book of Moses, Called Genesis*, trans. J. King (Edinburgh: Banner of Truth, 1965), 1:100.

To put this another way, Calvin believes that God not only wills good to us in Christ but that God's goodwill does not contradict itself in essence, even if it may seem to do so in human sight. Calvin is not a philosopher; he is a very practical theologian who bases knowledge of God on the gift of faith, not independent reason. Not all of God's will has been revealed to us, but we are concerned only with what has been revealed, and the rest is neither necessary for us nor any of our business. Everything that God has revealed must be believed as true, but there are different categories of biblical teaching. Some are the promises on which faith is established and the beliefs essential for salvation (3.2.29). Others are doctrines that are very important but about which amicably expressed differences can be tolerated; these points are not grounds for breaking Christian fellowship (4.1.12). Yet other teachings concern various aspects of life or practice, often expressed as general rules for corporate or personal behavior. In these latter circumstances, Christian freedom plays a vital role, because the precise ways that general rules are to be carried out are not specified.

To summarize: in order to understand Calvin's social and economic thought, one must remember that he is instructing and exhorting Christians, whom he assumes are existentially acquainted with God and therefore know that God is good and that God wills good for them, and that their highest good is to know and serve this good God. Knowledge that leads to salvation is conditioned by the experience of faith, but much social and economic truth can be and is known without saving faith. So it is possible to adapt what Calvin says on socioeconomic matters to address a non-Christian audience. Nonetheless, the presupposition of his teaching is that he is addressing Christians, the elect insofar as earthly sight can determine, and much of the cogency or beauty of his argument depends on accepting his axioms.

SOME DOCTRINES RELATED TO SOCIAL AND ECONOMIC LIFE

Understanding the interconnected group of doctrines on law, Christian life, and Christian freedom is important for making sense of Calvin's teachings on social and economic issues. These linked doctrines also illustrate the relationship between general principles or rules given in Scripture and the circumstantial applications that human beings must determine for themselves.

Law and the Decalogue

As is well known, for Calvin the Ten Commandments, which are summarized in Christ's two great commandments (Matt. 22:37–40), express God's unchanging will for God's people. Since the fall, human beings can no longer truly understand or practice the law by their natural abilities, although knowledge of the second table (the love of neighbors) has been less severely damaged than that of the first table (the worship of God). Calvin clearly acknowledges that special talents for social and economic life are part of God's created gifts to all humanity, including "good heathen" (2.2.12–17). Furthermore, he recognizes that honest pagans can keep the letter of the law in such matters as honoring parents, not killing or stealing, and so forth. However, in Calvin's view, neither the worship of God nor the love of the neighbor can be rightly done without the other, and thus real love of the neighbor is only possible for the redeemed who are moved by the grace of the Holy Spirit (3.7.4). Since he is addressing believers, when he explains the social and economic commandments, he focuses on what it means for Christians to fulfill them.

For Calvin, the "third" and principal use of the law is to serve Christians as a pattern for love, as a guide to the right way to love God and their neighbors (2.7.12). This third use is not simply a series of dos and don'ts; it encompasses a whole way of life. The two tables of the law can never be independent of each other, and thus socioeconomic matters are conditioned by, and even subsumed under, the primary service of God. Although the first table, the worship of God, always takes precedence over the second in principle, in actual practice the love of neighbor may be the best evidence for real love of God—better than the finest liturgy offered by a hypocritical heart. Logically, then, Calvin's teaching on the law demonstrates that social and economic behavior is neither an autonomous sphere of human life, nor just an optional addendum; it is a vital part of the Christian worship of God.[4]

The Genevan reformer is always practical, and he works to make it clear to his hearers that what he is saying is immediately relevant to them. To explain how Christians are to understand the law, Calvin gives examples. For instance, in the commandment forbidding murder, he shows what it means to practice the third use of the law:

> All violence, injury, and any harmful thing at all that may injure our neighbor's body are forbidden to us. We are accordingly commanded if we find anything of use to us in saving our neighbors' lives, faithfully to employ it: if there is anything that makes for their peace, to see to it; if anything harmful, to ward it off; if they are in any danger, to lend a helping hand. . . . Therefore this law also forbids murder of the heart, and enjoins the inner intent to save a brother's life. (2.8.40)

4. See Elsie Anne McKee, *John Calvin on the Diaconate and Liturgical Almsgiving* (Geneva: Droz, 1984), chap. 10.

Calvin's exposition of this commandment applies it in ways that are not obvious from the literal sense of the biblical text or the viewpoint of independent human reason, yet what he says is plainly in keeping with the intent of Jesus' summary of the law: "Love your neighbor as yourself."

Christian Life and Christian Freedom

When Calvin describes the Christian life, one key issue is how believers are to value and use the present earthly life, especially by comparison with the future life. Repeatedly Calvin insists that although the future life is of course better—it is free from sin and the cares and crosses of this world—nonetheless that future glory should never lead the Christian to regard this earthly life as evil. Meditation on the future life should relativize the value placed on this world, but that should not lead to despising the earthly. On the contrary, although by comparison with the life to come the present life is much less good and blessed, nevertheless, because it is the gift of the good Creator who is also the Redeemer, this life is still good and blessed. Calvin, so often pictured as a killjoy, in fact praises the many wonderful things God has given for human enjoyment as well as human use:

> [God] meant not only to provide for necessity but also for delight and good cheer. . . . Has the Lord clothed the flowers with the great beauty that greets our eyes, the sweetness of smell that is wafted upon our nostrils, and yet will it be unlawful for our eyes to be affected by that beauty, or our sense of smell by the sweetness of that odor? What? Did he not so distinguish colors as to make some more lovely than others? What? Did he not endow gold and silver, ivory and marble, with a loveliness that renders them more precious than other metals or stones? Did he not, in short, render many things attractive to us, apart from their necessary use? (3.10.2)

For Calvin, the wonder of God's generosity and the beauty of God's creation, combined with God's will for human good, give us many reasons to delight in that divine goodness which lavishes gifts on all human beings.

The one condition for using and enjoying God's good gifts in this earthly life is that they be used and enjoyed rightly, that is, according to the purposes for which God gave them. Calvin says that God gave us such blessings "for our good, not for our ruin" (3.10.2) and that what constitutes "our good" is, for believers, conditioned by the two great commandments. In the first place, material blessings are rightly used when they serve as means to fulfill the purpose of human existence, which is worshiping God in word and life: "One bridle is put upon [our free use of God's gifts] if it be determined that all things were created for us that we might recognize the Author and give thanks for his kindness toward us" (3.10.3). Right use of God's generosity means both thankfully acknowledging the Giver and demonstrating that gratitude by being responsible stewards of the blessings. If we abuse the gifts, we dishonor the Giver and fail in our earthly vocation: "Where is your thanksgiving if you so gorge yourself with banqueting or wine that you either become stupid or are rendered useless for the duties of piety and of your calling?" (3.10.3).

The second dimension of right use of material things is guided by the second great commandment, employing God's gifts to serve the love of neighbors:

> But scripture . . . warns that whatever benefits we obtain from the Lord have been entrusted to us on this condition: that they be applied to the common good of the church. And therefore the lawful use of all benefits consists in a liberal and kindly sharing of them with others. . . . Let this, therefore, be our rule for generosity and beneficence: We are the stewards of everything God has conferred on us by which we are able to help our neighbor, and are required to render account of our stewardship. Moreover, the only right stewardship is that which is tested by the rule of love. (3.7.5)

In fact, any use of the wealth that God has entrusted to human beings that does not follow these conditions is an offense against both commandments:

> God then, no doubt, is deprived by us of his right, when we are unkind to the poor, and refuse them aid in their necessity. We indeed thereby wrong human beings, and are cruel; but our crime is still more heinous, inasmuch as we are unfaithful stewards. God is more liberal to us than to others so that some portion of our abundance may come to the poor.
>
> God consecrates to their use the things which he has given us so abundantly, so we become guilty of sacrilege whenever we do not give to our brethren what God commands us.[5]

Furthermore, Calvin deals with the cavil that what we have earned is our own possession, as if we had not received it. He insists that whatever we have "is a simple and free gift of God, however it may come to us, even when it would seem to have been obtained by our own skill and diligence, and supplied by our own hands. For it is by his blessing alone that our labors truly prosper" (3.20.44).

In every way, Calvin emphasizes both God's amazing generosity in giving people all that they need for this earthly life and the corresponding sober enjoyment by which Christians show their appreciation for these gifts and

5. Calvin, *Commentaries on the Minor Prophets* (Grand Rapids: Eerdmans, 1950), 586. I have made slight modifications to wording and punctuation for clarity.

never forget either the Giver or the appointed role of the gifts in Christian life. However, says Calvin, Scripture does not give Christians detailed instructions in the use of their material possessions:

> God certainly always commands that we relieve our brethren's necessities, but He nowhere lays it down how much we ought to give, so that we can make a calculation and divide between ourselves and the poor. He nowhere binds us to specific times or persons or places but simply bids us be guided by the rule of love.[6]

The "rule of love" is a rather general guide, so how much should one give? Calvin believes that giving is not limited to sharing our profits or what is superfluous for our own needs: "We are not to spare our capital funds, if the interest available from these fails to meet the necessities [of the poor]. In other words, your liberality has to go as far as the diminution of your patrimony, and the disposal of your estates."[7] On the other hand, the value of the gift is not measured by its amount. While there is no absolute standard of measure, what matters is the attitude of the giver, and when offered in the right spirit, any gift is honored. If "the poor person has a liberal mind, . . . a small gift is looked upon as a rich and generous sacrifice."[8]

By the general rule of love, each Christian has both considerable freedom and inescapable responsibility to decide the day-to-day embodiment of earthly stewardship not in a legalistic way but according to the Holy Spirit's guidance. Implicit here is the idea that one cannot give a certain amount and wash his or her hands of the poor. The rule of love must be held constantly in mind; in each new situation, one must assess what the loving response to the neighbor should be in this concrete time and place. Practical as always, Calvin acknowledges that the scope of the obligation and the personal reach of the Christian may well not be the same:

> There is a general command to relieve the need of all the poor [and not just some]. Yet those who succor the indigence of those whom they know or see to be suffering are obeying this law, even though they overlook many who are pressed by equally great needs, because either they cannot know all or cannot provide for all. (3.20.39)

6. Calvin, *Commentary on the Second Epistle of Paul the Apostle to the Corinthians and the Epistles to Timothy, Titus, and Philemon*, trans. T. A. Smail, ed. D. and T. Torrance (Edinburgh: St. Andrew, 1964), 110.

7. Calvin, *Commentary on the Harmony of the Gospels, Matthew, Mark, and Luke*, trans. A. W. Morrison, ed. D. and T. Torrance (Edinburgh: St. Andrew, 1972), 216.

8. Calvin, *Commentary on the Acts of the Apostles, 1–13*, trans. J. F. Fraser and W. J. G. McDonald, ed. D. and T. Torrance (Edinburgh: St. Andrew, 1965), 334.

The rule of love is universal; the concrete daily application is immediate and local.

The modern West is most concerned with individual rights and obligations, but in Calvin's own age the West (like many parts of the world today) was more deeply impressed with corporate privileges and responsibilities. Thus, Calvin recognizes that not only do God's laws apply to whole societies as well as individuals, but these societies also have a certain freedom in implementing the corporate application of God's teaching with regard to social and economic issues. Calvin the trained lawyer does not regard the judicial laws of ancient Israel to be obligatory for other societies, but the fundamental principles of equity these Old Testament laws express are universal, and those principles must always be maintained (4.20.15–16). For example, all people know through their consciences that murder should be punished, but the nature of the punishment may vary from country to country or age to age. Different jurisdictions have the right to determine the exact penalty for a crime, but then the individual members of the society are bound to those specific regulations, not by conscience but for order and decency.

In similar fashion there is freedom in the administration of all God's earthly blessings, but Christian societies may use these material goods in various ways. The purpose for which God gave the gifts must always be kept in view, and God's rule of justice ("equity") must be maintained, but details may vary in different places. For example, a government may determine whether to allow usury (loaning money at interest) under certain circumstances and not others. Calvin allows the legitimacy of a 5 percent interest rate in particular business projects where no one's livelihood is endangered; however, no loans at interest may be charged to poor people who must borrow to live.[9] The application of the principle of equity must be tailored to the concrete situation. The principles are universal; the application is particular.

SOME PERSPECTIVES ON HUMAN LIFE RELATED TO SOCIAL AND ECONOMIC ISSUES

The discussion of law, Christian life, and Christian freedom gives a good idea of how social and economic issues are interwoven in some of Calvin's fundamental teachings. A second set of doctrines that are significant (though less commonly explained) center on the reformer's understanding of the character of human society.

9. See Georgia Harkness, *John Calvin: The Man and His Ethics* (1931; repr., Nashville: Abingdon, 1958), 201–10.

Human Society, Marriage, and Diverse Gifts

One of the basic grounds for Calvin's social teaching is the conviction that Adam and Eve and all their descendants were created to be social beings. His commentaries and sermons on Genesis, especially Gen. 2:18–21, as well as statements in the *Institutes*, repeatedly make this idea clear: "The commencement [of creation], therefore, involves a general principle, that man was formed to be a social animal."[10] Indeed, Calvin takes for granted that human beings cannot be happy in isolation.

> [Even though Adam had the animals,] yet he always remained as if half a person, incomplete [until God created Eve]. . . . For there is nothing more contrary to our nature than solitude, as each one knows. If we had everything we could wish, a table in front of us all day long, our bed ready for us to sleep, if we had both accessories and all necessities; if then each one had an earthly paradise on condition that he live there alone, would that life not be like being half dead? We would do nothing but languish in the midst of such felicities—each one knows that.[11]

The paradigmatic pattern of human society is the companionship of Adam and Eve, the married couple. Calvin praises the happiness and fruits of this "truly celestial order"[12] when it is rightly maintained:

> [If Adam had not fallen,] we would see that God reigns over marriage: He was the author of it, and He blesses everything so that it would be like an angelic melody between husbands and wives. And that would be so not only for a married couple themselves, but neighbors would help each other, and each woman would draw her neighbors and relations to do their duty, and each husband the same. See then, there would be a general covenant [*alliance*] of God's grace in this world, if our father Adam had not sinned.[13]

Despite the fall, Calvin understands marriage, this God-given association, as a basis for human unity because all humans are related—they all came from the same original family:

> God's inestimable goodness and His more than fatherly care is demonstrated in this place, when He did not want man to be alone but wanted him to have company. That order was established in such a way as to warn us by the creation of Eve that, being thus formed from our father

10. Calvin, *Commentaries on the First Book of Moses*, 1:128.
11. Calvin, *Sermons sur la Genèse chapitres 1,1–11,4*, ed. Max Engammare (Neukirchen-Vluyn: Neukirchener Verlag, 2000), 125–126. Translations by the author.
12. Ibid., 138.
13. Ibid., 129.

> Adam and procreated of his seed, we must truly be one. Let each one recognize his neighbors as his flesh and bone, and his very substance.[14]

Marriage and the unity of the human family have been damaged by sin and the fall, but both still remain God's good gifts, and in Christ there is restoration of both marriage and society. It is notable that almost every time Calvin discusses a passage on marriage he includes a reference to the larger community of the human race, and sometimes he gives this "implication" of the covenant of marriage more attention than the relationship between man and woman. Not every person is married, but every person is clearly part of the human family and community.[15]

Human beings were not only intended to live together for their happiness, but they also need each other. In commentaries on various New Testament passages that list diverse charisms (e.g., Rom. 12, 1 Cor. 12), Calvin emphasizes that God has given different people different gifts. Here the focus is not material possessions but human abilities. One purpose for this diversity of abilities is to draw people together, so that each might help the others:

> Here . . . [Paul] is instructing individuals to bring what they have as a contribution to the common stock, and not to keep the gifts of God to themselves, which would mean that the benefits of each person's gifts would be restricted to himself alone, instead of being shared with others; but [they are] to work harmoniously together for the edification of all.[16]

The diverse gifts also ensure that every human being needs other people. To put it another way, no one has so much that he or she can stand alone.

> All [people] desire to have enough to prevent them from needing help from their brethren. But there is a bond of fellowship when no one has sufficient for himself, but is forced to borrow from others. . . . To prevent anyone from being grieved that he has not been given everything, [Paul] reminds us that each individual has his own responsibility assigned to him by the good purpose of God, because it is expedient for the common salvation of the body that no individual should be so furnished with the fulness of gifts as to despise his brethren with impunity.[17]

14. Ibid., 126.

15. Ibid., 134, 136, 137.

16. Calvin, *Commentary on the First Epistle of Paul the Apostle to the Corinthians*, trans. J. W. Fraser, ed. D. and T. Torrance (Edinburgh: St. Andrew, 1960), 260.

17. Calvin, *Commentary on the Epistles of Paul the Apostle to the Romans and to the Thessalonians*, trans. R. Mackenzie, ed. D. and T. Torrance (Edinburgh: St. Andrew, 1961), 268.

If everyone values and uses rightly both his or her own gifts and those of others, then the community of faith will serve God in harmony. If, though, individuals are not satisfied to use their own (limited) gifts appropriately, the result will be detrimental to the gifts as well as the community:

> All things are not appropriate for all people, but the gifts of God are so distributed that each has a limited portion. Each individual ought to be so intent upon bestowing his own gifts for the edification of the church, that no one may relinquish his own function, and trespass on that of another. . . . All gifts have their own appointed limits, and to depart from them is to spoil the gifts themselves.[18]

As we have seen, in the sermons on Genesis Calvin expresses awareness of the happiness and strength that human beings can draw from God's plan for human association in families and communities. In dealing with the passages on charisms he points out that selfish independence is restrained by mutual dependence, and people truly enjoy their individual gifts when they use them to contribute to the common life according to the purposes God intended. Whether his emphasis is on gratitude or respect for necessary constraints, it is evident that Calvin was convinced that no person could or should live for himself or herself, nor can any solitary person truly fulfill God's will for humanity.

To say that people are created as social beings is not to say that all are equal. Calvin certainly affirms that both women and men are made in God's image and that both masters and servants are among the elect. However, he believed that God established hierarchies for this earthly life, and these mundane differences of rank or authority are therefore right and as permanent as this earth. Thus, women are subordinate to men, children to parents, servants to masters, citizens or subjects to magistrates or kings. Each person is called to live according to God's will in his or her own work, station, or task. That means the exercise of just authority or sincere obedience, and the appropriate use of all gifts according to each one's vocation and estate.

Humanity and Nature

Human beings were created to be stewards of God's world as well as a family made in God's image. Calvin's hierarchical views mean that the nature of dominion is different for women than for men, but it is clear that he considers ruling over nature and caring for it the common responsibility of men and women. The critical issue is responsibility. Susan Schreiner has demonstrated

18. Ibid.

that Calvin does not confine his attention to nature simply to its relationship to human beings, but that does remain his primary focus.[19]

In one sense, it could be said that Calvin's most immediate interest in the natural world is how that "theater of God's glory" is related to believers. Nature is the most visible arena of God's power. In early modern Europe (as was true long before and still is in many parts of the world today), the power of nature was not always obviously benevolent. In fact, it was and is one source of anxiety and suffering. Thus Calvin, who is speaking to Christians, emphasizes that piety and faith concentrate on the manifestation of God's power for believers' good (3.2.31). The mighty Creator is the same God whom persons of faith know as the Redeemer. And so, because God has chosen to give them eternal salvation, believers know that God's governing care (providence) also is only for their good. None of the accidents of this world, which because of sin they have not learned to manage according to God's intent, can separate them from God. A world that may appear to be out of control can hurt believers in their earthly lives, but nothing can finally or essentially harm those whom God has redeemed and called. That is, Christians who live in this often dangerous world are not in any *ultimate* danger.

That said, the responsibility of caring for all who suffer in this earthly life rests on believers by God's command and gift. The points examined above—Calvin's teaching on the third use of the law as a guide for regenerate Christians, Christian freedom in the life of faith, and individual responsibility to love and serve God and neighbor—all manifest his intense interest in the personal character of each believer's relationship with God and each believer's faithful response to the social and economic teaching of the Bible. However, personal does not mean individualistic. Every Christian is called to live as part of the human family according to God's original intent, a vocation to which believers are restored by Christ's grace. Every Christian is called to exercise right stewardship in all of God's world, sharing with those in need, enjoying God's material blessings precisely insofar as they honor God's purposes, and caring for God's world as good stewards. But individual Christians are Christians only as part of the body of Christ, the church.

CORPORATE ECCLESIAL EXPRESSIONS OF SOCIAL AND ECONOMIC LIFE

The body of Christ visible on earth must also be shaped by God's will for righteousness in social and economic life, and that God-directedness applies to all dimensions of its life—liturgical, structural, and practical.

19. See Susan E. Schreiner, *The Theater of His Glory: Nature and the Natural Order in the Thought of John Calvin* (Grand Rapids: Baker Academic, 1991). The last clause represents my interpretation and not Schreiner's.

Worship

In keeping with the fact that Calvin is addressing Christians, there is an important role for social and economic issues in the context of worship, through individual prayer but also and perhaps especially in the gathered community of faith. In Acts 2:42, the paradigmatic Reformed description of right corporate worship, there are four elements: preaching of the Word, the Lord's Supper, prayers, and *koinonia*. Of these, the last two are directly concerned with social or economic matters in one way or another.[20]

Prayers in the liturgy naturally focus on the praise of God and acknowledgment of personal and corporate sinfulness, including abuse of God's gifts and wrongs done to God's people. The Calvinist confession of sin is too well known to need further attention, but the intensity of Calvin's concern for intercessory prayer is often forgotten and worth emphasizing. Prayers are one of the most important means of remembering and asking for restoration of the social ties of the Christian family, and even for the good of "all people who live on earth," as Calvin says in explaining the Lord's Prayer:

> Now if we so desire, as is fitting, to extend our hand to one another and to help one another, there is nothing in which we can benefit our brethren more than in commending them to the providential care of the best of fathers; for if [God] is kind and favorable, nothing at all else can be desired. Indeed, we owe even this very thing to our Father. Just as one who truly and deeply loves any father of a family at the same time embraces his whole household with love and good will, so it becomes us in like measure to show to his people, to his family, and lastly, to his inheritance, the same zeal and affection that we have toward this Heavenly Father. For he so honored these as to call them the fullness of his only-begotten Son. Let the Christian [person], then, conform his prayers to this rule in order that they may be in common and embrace all who are his brothers [and sisters] in Christ, not only those whom he at present sees and recognizes as such but all [people] who dwell on earth. For what God has determined concerning them is beyond our knowing except that it is no less godly than humane to wish and hope the best for them. (3.20.38)

In the Sunday liturgy, following the instructions of 1 Timothy 2:1, there were formal prayers for all states of humanity: civil leaders; ministers of the church; the sick, needy, and afflicted; and all on earth.[21]

Special evidence for the seriousness with which Calvin regarded repentance and intercession is seen in his creation of the day of prayer service. This

20. See McKee, *John Calvin on the Diaconate*, chap. 3.

21. See Calvin, "The Lord's Day Service with Lord's Supper," in *John Calvin: Writings on Pastoral Piety*, ed. and trans. Elsie Anne McKee (Mahwah, NJ: Paulist Press, 2001), 126–31.

established a weekly liturgical reminder of God's providential immediacy in believers' lives and the prayers that Christian brothers and sisters owe on each other's behalf. Daily services also included petitions for the afflicted; those who knew of illness or other problems were encouraged to tell the preacher about these ills so that these sisters and brothers might be mentioned by name. In addition, a model prayer included in the catechism focused on those suffering persecution.[22] All of these forms of prayer—whether naming a sick parishioner, or remembering women and men in captivity for their faith, or asking forgiveness for failures to care for neighbors, or giving thanks for a victory by beleaguered fellow Protestants—were a part of the social consciousness of Calvin's worshiping community.

The other element of Acts 2:42 that links formal worship with social and economic issues in concrete ways is *koinonia*, or mutual fellowship. The forms that *koinonia* can take are not dictated by the verse, but Calvin's familiarity with Scripture led him to identify almsgiving as the primary liturgical expression of mutual fellowship. He also saw the apostolic kiss of peace as a manifestation of *koinonia* (though apparently not one he wanted to practice in Geneva). The alms offering, money for the support of the poor and needy, was usually associated with the Lord's Supper. It was an expression of thanksgiving to God and of the mutual love that being spiritually fed in Christ's body and blood should nourish among earthly members of his body. The material offerings in worship were not only a form of gratitude to God but also a practical means for God's service in the world. In areas where the Calvinist church was not established, these voluntary collections might well be the only funds available for the work of the diaconate.[23]

Church Constitution and Ministries

It has long been recognized that the Reformed tradition shaped by Calvin includes four ecclesiastical offices—elders, deacons, teachers, and pastors—in its understanding of New Testament church order. Three of these—the diaconate, the consistory, and the office of doctor—were the institutional structures Calvin established to embody the corporate responsibility of the church

22. Calvin, "Weekday Worship: The Day of Prayer Liturgy" in McKee, *John Calvin*, 157–177. The importance of the day of prayer service is revealed by the fact that it was the only one besides the Sunday morning service for which Calvin wrote a special liturgy, and the only day besides Sunday that was observed with a partial holiday and services at two different hours so that everyone could attend. For daily services and prayer for the persecuted, see ibid., 152, 215–17.

23. See Elsie Anne McKee, *Diakonia in the Classical Reformed Tradition and Today* (Grand Rapids: Eerdmans, 1988), 31–33.

for social and economic issues. Christian care for the poor, education for this life and especially in the faith, and oversight of the people to build up their confession and life as Christians were certainly not new ideas. However, the way Calvin structured these Christian responsibilities, particularly the two "lay" offices of elder and deacon, was new and distinctive.

According to his reading of the New Testament, Calvin believed that the church should have an office of oversight or discipline—what might be called "Christian formation." This task was to be exercised not by one bishop but by a plurality of representative church leaders made up of two kinds of presbyters (pastors and elders) who formed the consistory. The work of oversight was concerned with helping to shape believers in the marks of Christians: the confession of faith, a life which is fitting, and participation in the sacraments of the church (4.1.8). In conjunction with the preaching of the gospel, the consistory was intended to bring to repentance those who disregarded the knowledge and practice of faith, and of morality and justice. As Robert Kingdon has so clearly shown, this discipline was not the harsh series of continual excommunications often caricatured in older accounts of Calvin's Geneva. The consistory was rather what he deftly calls a "compulsory counseling service," which worked diligently to correct and reconcile those who were at odds, for the sake of God's honor and building up the Christian community.[24] In a sense, the elders and pastors together focused on the work of making the earthly society in their charge approximate as closely as possible God's purpose for humanity: to create Adam and Eve and their descendants as social beings whose good it is to live in right fellowship with God and each other.

The diaconate was Calvin's other lay ecclesiastical office. Its responsibility was to care for all those who could not care for themselves, such as orphans, widows, and the handicapped. Calvin's sermons clearly demonstrate his conviction that this office is biblical and normative:

> Sometimes it is considered an office of small importance to serve God by serving the poor. But St. Paul says that it is an excellent rank, indeed a freedom in the faith to those who have walked rightly in this task. Thus, therefore, we can apply St. Paul's passage [1 Tim. 3:8–13] to St. Luke's discussion [Acts 6:1–6], and see that it does not merely tell us a story about what was done once, but it shows us that this ought to be a lasting order in the Church of God. . . . God is informing us what

24. Robert M. Kingdon, "Calvin and the Family: The Work of the Consistory in Geneva," in *Calvin's Work in Geneva*, ed. R. Gamble (New York: Garland, 1992), 96. See also other writings by Kingdon and his group of graduates who have worked on Consistory records, such as Jeffrey Watt and Thomas Lambert. For Calvin's theological reasoning with regard to the eldership, see Elsie Anne McKee, *Elders and the Plural Ministry* (Geneva: Droz, 1988).

> government, order, and organization He commands there to be among His people. If we want to be considered His Church we must have what is here proclaimed to us. What the apostles did [in Acts 6] must be a lasting example to us, since we have a general rule about it from the mouth of St. Paul. . . . It is necessary that the poor be cared for, and for this there must be deacons.[25]

The function comes first, then the office and personnel to carry out the task. Care for the poor is one of the responsibilities of the church as a body, and therefore the Holy Spirit led the apostles to establish deacons.

Calvin's diaconate, like the eldership, was made up of a plurality of persons and a variety of functions. (Calvin always prefers corporate leadership, especially in the church. Even when it is applied by one or two people, the authority is always held by a plurality of individuals.) In principle, male deacons were to collect and administer the church's financial aid for the poor, and female deacons were to nurse and tend the afflicted in person. (In Geneva the "nursing" ministry was headed by a man, and Calvin flatly stated that this was not right, but he seems to have concluded that since the function was being carried out, he would tolerate the deviation from the biblically preferred personnel.[26]) The diaconate is concerned with seeing that those who suffer from physical ills are provided with the care that God's children owe to each other as members of the same family. It is also the church's corporate economic and social ministry in the stewardship of material goods for the love of the neighbor.[27]

What is significant here is that these two offices, the eldership and the diaconate, demonstrate Calvin's conviction that the church as an earthly institution has corporate responsibility for social and economic issues. Individuals are to work for right relationships and economic justice in their own lives, but the church itself also has biblically grounded structures concerned with shaping good Christian lives and a just Christian society. That means the church as institution has responsibilities to those who need encouragement or rebuke, and those who need food or shelter or education or medicine, in order that they may receive what they require to honor God and live in truly human fellowship.

The Body of Christ in the Inhabited World

Calvin's commitment to the international, ecumenical character of the church yielded a significant dimension of his thinking about social and economic prac-

25. From Calvin's sermon on Acts 6:1–3, quoted in McKee, *John Calvin on the Diaconate*, 156.

26. See the passage from his sermon on 1 Tim. 5:9–10, quoted in McKee, *John Calvin on the Diaconate*, 215–16.

27. See McKee, *Diakonia in the Classical Reformed Tradition*, esp. 61–82.

tice. Several forms of this international church life may be identified briefly. One is Calvin's attention to education, which included the establishment of an ecclesiastical office of doctor or teacher. Although this educational interest may seem to modern Christians tangentially related to the social and economic life of the church, in early modern Europe it contributed significantly to the "multicultural" (or extralocal) social links among Reformed people.[28] The founding of the Genevan Academy was an important part of creating an international network of European leaders, which helped shape a new kind of religious (confessional) connectionalism.

In its own way, this Reformed family of churches replaced the universal structure of Rome with a network of churches, geographically separate, each possessing its own confession. The network was intended to be both mutually supportive and mutually correcting, a family in which there was room for some diversity in a common communion. Something of this sense of community is found in Calvin's description of the purpose of catechisms, which are "public testimonies by which Churches, that agree in Christian doctrine though widely separated in space, may mutually recognize each other."[29] The word "mutually" is significant: one does not dictate to the other, there is a willingness to accept differences on some matters provided these are not held with contentious obstinacy (4.1.12), but there is mutual recognition as fellow members of the faith. This mutuality included consultations among the Reformed churches, and in this as in many other ways, Calvin was building on the work of Martin Bucer and his colleagues. One vital example, begun in the first generation and extending for many years, was the exchange of worship practices and borrowing of liturgical materials and Psalters.[30] The correspondence between Geneva and

28. Calvin's doctors were fundamentally concerned with the purpose of keeping the doctrine of the Christian community pure and bringing each new generation up in the knowledge of God. This included both elementary and more advanced levels of humanist learning as well as theological training. The highest rank of doctors, the "public lecturers" who taught theology and philosophy, were recognized as ministers of the church. The primary focus of the ministry of education was providing for the future leadership of the church, though at times (especially after Calvin's day) there might have been some disagreement about whether that meant essentially pastors or also included Christian civil leaders. If the latter, then the element of social sharing would be strengthened even beyond the church. See Robert W. Henderson, *The Teaching Office in the Reformed Tradition* (Philadelphia: Westminster, 1962), and Karin Maag, *Seminary or University? The Genevan Academy and Reformed Higher Education, 1559–1620* (Brookfield, NH: Ashgate, 1995).

29. "John Calvin to the Faithful Ministers . . . ," prefatory letter to "Catechism of the Church of Geneva," 89. There are various collections of Reformed confessions and catechisms, which testify to the desire to respect national, regional, or cultural entities. The contrast with the single Augsburg Confession for all Lutheran churches is striking.

30. See H. O. Old, *The Patristic Roots of Reformed Worship* (Zurich: TVZ, 1975).

the Swiss and South German churches in deciding how to handle the Servetus case and the later Synod of Dort provide other examples. Together these illustrate the common Reformed conviction that corporate members of the body of Christ are mutually accountable to each other as corporate groups, just as individual members of Christ are accountable to each other.

Intra-Reformed church witness is balanced by ecclesiastical witness to the world, particularly in action for justice—individual and corporate service in the political realm as an expression of Christian faithfulness. This can perhaps be likened to Calvin's comments on the use of charisms to serve the common good—gifts that include the power to influence others. For example, religious refugees must be helped, not only with material means to survive and to earn their livelihood but also with political assistance to enable them to find justice. Calvin quite clearly believed that active, forceful resistance to injustice perpetrated by earthly rulers can only be legitimated in a *regular* way when it is led by "lesser magistrates" (4.20.30–31). However, recognizing the honor that should properly be accorded to divinely constituted authority does not exclude individual or corporate political efforts to dissuade persecutors, as Calvin's own example demonstrates.

When the court of Francis I was devastating villages of evangelical believers in southeastern France in 1544–1545, Calvin encouraged the Genevan government to welcome the refugees, care for their sick, and employ the healthy. However, he also made a long journey and wrote many letters to Swiss Protestant governments and leaders in an effort to get the latter to intercede with the French king. As he wrote to Heinrich Bullinger on November 24, 1544, "What can we do, therefore, but strain every nerve that these godly brethren may not, through our shortcoming in duty, become the victims of such cruelty, and that the door may not for a long time be shut against Christ?"[31] In similar fashion he supported the efforts of a Protestant merchant who was seeking to free some Protestants imprisoned in Lyons:

> It is said that they who comfort the children of God in their persecutions which they endure for the gospel are fellow laborers for the truth. Be content with this testimony, for it is no light matter that God should uphold and approve us as His martyrs even though we do not personally suffer, merely because His martyrs are helped and comforted by us.[32]

The same idea is expressed more fully and more broadly in the *Institutes*, where Calvin expands the recipients of Christian intervention from those who suffer religious persecution to all innocent victims of injustice:

31. See McKee, *John Calvin*, 317.
32. Ibid., 323.

> I say that not only they who labor for the defense of the gospel but they who in any way maintain the cause of righteousness suffer persecution for righteousness. Therefore, whether in declaring God's truth against Satan's falsehoods or in taking up the protection of the good and the innocent against the wrongs of the wicked, we must undergo the offenses and hatred of the world, which may imperil either our life, our fortunes, or our honor. Let us not grieve or be troubled in thus far devoting our efforts to God, or count ourselves miserable in those matters in which he has with his own lips declared us blessed [Matt. 5:10]. (3.8.7)

These words demonstrate how the biblical injunctions about the right use of everything that God has given (life, fortune, honor), and the right participation in the human family that God created as our earthly community and comfort, should fit together. Defending the faith and protecting the innocent are both expressions of "maintain[ing] the cause of righteousness" and devoting oneself to God, and any suffering incurred should be considered a blessing because it is "persecution for righteousness." This quotation may well sum up these reflections on the dynamic, profoundly religious character of Calvin's teaching on social and economic matters.

THE SIGNIFICANCE OF CALVIN'S SOCIAL AND ECONOMIC TEACHING IN HIS DAY

The Role of the "Mundane" in Calvin's Theology

One of the first points to strike the modern Christian may be the integral way in which Calvin's thought on these apparently mundane issues, such as food for the hungry, economic justice for the poor, stewardship of God's gifts, good family relationships, and so forth, is inextricably interwoven with the fundamental principles of his theology. Social and economic matters are not an addendum to the worship of God; they are part and parcel of right earthly worship. No sixteenth-century persons who followed Calvin's theology would ever be able to separate how they ruled their subjects, nursed their sick neighbors, priced the goods in their shops, or obeyed their parents or disciplined their children from their relationship to God. God always comes first, but the honor owed to God is often most clearly manifested in how believers live their day-to-day vocations. Right worship should be expressed in prayer and praise—hearing God's word, receiving the gift of the sacraments, and giving material aid for the needy. It should also be expressed in the home and the marketplace, in city council and business activities, in care for the refugee and the poor and afflicted, in fair working conditions and just wages and conscientious labor.

To the sixteenth-century European this necessary interrelationship of theology and ethics, of love for God and for the neighbor, would not have appeared strange. What would have been distinctive in Calvin's version of the common biblical teaching was the constructive character and intensity with which he insisted on the indivisible connection between right worship of God and right living as a social and economic being. One of his recurrent phrases is *negotium cum Deo*, "in every detail of life it is with God that we have to do" (e.g., 1.17.2; 3.3.6, 16; 3.7.2). The quasi-economic language is notable, though Calvin does *not* mean bargaining with God. In effect, what he is saying is that there is no moment or facet of believers' existence that is not present to God's sight. Thus, every instant, every aspect of their lives—which they were created to live as social beings in an earthly world—every human relationship and every economic act must be done as in God's presence. That can seem like a constant state of accounting for oneself, but it is also meant as a gift: no person is too humble to belong to God, no act is too small to honor God, no aspect of human life dedicated to God is without meaning.

The energy this teaching gave to Calvinists has led to all kinds of controversy. It is vital here to recognize—and reclaim—how Calvin himself understood the relationship between the service of God and life in God's world, and what he would regard as evidence of success. Calvin recognizes in a matter-of-fact way that the earthly fruit of faith in God might well not look very successful in worldly terms: "For whoever the Lord has adopted and deemed worthy of his fellowship ought to prepare themselves for a hard, toilsome, and unquiet life, crammed with very many and various kinds of evil" (3.8.1). (In fact, unbelievers will often experience earthly success far more than the elect will.) Enjoying God's good creation is appropriate, having enough for one's daily vocation is good, but those are expressions of earthly blessings, not marks of ultimate success. What faith actually promises the believer is the certainty "that, however many things may fail us that have to do with the maintenance of this life, God will never fail" (3.2.28). Calvin's chief interest is that ultimate success defined as right relationship with God. Such success is measured by faith and love and nothing else.

This revaluing of Christian character had important consequences. The Calvinist conviction that the action of the smallest child or humblest servant, prompted by faith and expressing love, is counted as a worthwhile contribution to God's service, resulted in a dynamic sense of personal and corporate responsibility and power. As long as it was embedded in and conditioned by the teaching that God may grant earthly goods but is primarily concerned with the ultimate good of human beings, this energy could shape Christian life as Calvin envisioned it. For Calvin, having God's goodwill and being engrafted into Christ (his earthly cross as well as his final resurrection) *is* success for the

Christian, and all material wealth and human relationships must be lived in accordance with that criterion of what is good and right and desirable. No one who heard Calvin thundering about human abuses of God's gifts, no one who heard him praying about the eschatological hope in Christ, would easily forget the conditions for the right use of God's great generosity in the present life, and the real character of Christian success.

Church/Corporate Responsibility for Social and Economic Life

Another aspect of Calvin's teaching on social and economic matters that had great significance for his own day and later is the way that Calvin understood these issues to be necessary parts of the constitution and responsibility of the church. His view of the role of education in the larger Christian world led to the establishment of an office of doctors and also helped to rebuild an international, shared consciousness in a fragmented Christendom. More concretely, Calvin's doctrine of the ministries of discipline or oversight and care for the needy led to his formulation of two previously unknown "lay ecclesiastical" offices—the eldership and the diaconate. The view of the activities of oversight and care of the poor as Christian ministries was a common Protestant teaching. The organization of these functions into necessary offices of the church as church, distinct from the civil authority, is a particular contribution of Calvin's (built on the work of Johannes Oecolampadius and Martin Bucer, but strengthened, clarified, established, and made practicable by the Genevan reformer).

In effect, these extraliturgical ecclesiastical offices gave to the Calvinist Reformed church a definite corporate means of expressing the responsibility of the church for the social and economic life of believers and of encouraging intellectual and cultural sharing on a larger scale. Looked at from the inside, how Christians handle human relationships and economic justice is not a matter of individual preference; all believers are necessarily part of a larger body that has the obligation to guide, train, rebuke, encourage, support, and teach each member. Looked at from the outside, the church has the continual responsibility to be actively involved in the social, economic, and educational realities of the world in which it lives. It is the corporate body of Christ on earth, and thus it is necessarily concerned with all dimensions of earthly life as an extension of its proclamation of the gospel.

CAUTION BY WAY OF CONCLUSION

One final note may be useful. In assessing what Calvin says and does not say, it is important to bear in mind the differences between his age and the present. To a modern Western audience, one of the most obvious differences is Calvin's traditional emphasis on hierarchy, between men and women as well as in society generally. (Hierarchical organization continues to be very important in more traditional societies, but almost all communities are affected by the challenge to hierarchy as an ideal.) Another difference is Calvin's limited awareness of the systemic character of economic oppression and intellectual hegemony. What happens today—for example, the unjust stranglehold of North on South in an industrialized global village and the Eurocentric definitions of what constitutes real scholarship—is far removed from the preindustrial and rather insular society of sixteenth-century Western Europe. A third difference is the extent of the havoc human beings have wreaked on God's creation by means of technology Calvin could never have imagined. A fourth difference is the amazing and growing pluralism and secularism of the twenty-first century, which demand that social and economic justice be considered in a religious and intellectual context that might well have horrified Calvin. All these differences must be taken seriously. Yet within its limits, Calvin's thought on social and economic issues, shaped by the conviction that the Redeemer God is also the Giver of the human society and earthly blessings that human beings enjoy and for which they are accountable, still has much to offer to those who read it with religious sensitivity and historical care.

2

Calvin and Church Discipline

Robert M. Kingdon

In this essay I want to advance and defend the proposition that in assessing John Calvin's impact on Reformed social and economic witness one needs to consider not only Calvin's ideas but also his activities. Calvin was not only a widely published scholar; he was also an active pastor. When we look at Calvin as a pastor, we discover his strong commitment to church discipline. We discover, furthermore, that this commitment had an enduring impact on Reformed churches all over the world. This is something that is distinctive about Calvinism, that separates it from such other varieties of Protestantism as Lutheranism and Zwinglianism. I realize that this takes us beyond the ideas André Biéler has examined in such a magistral way in his splendid analyses *La pensée économique et sociale de Calvin* (1959) and *L'homme et la femme dans la morale calviniste* (1963). But I think this is necessary if we are going to appreciate fully the nature of Calvin's impact on society and economy.

When Calvin returned to Geneva in 1541, to assume leadership of the entire Reformed church in this community, he bargained hard and insisted on two things. He insisted that Geneva must institute a form of catechism to be sure that the entire community could understand Christian doctrine. And he insisted that Geneva must establish a form of discipline to be sure that the entire community behave in a Christian way. Soon after he arrived, he drafted a catechism for Geneva, a catechism significantly revised from the one he had drafted for the community back in 1537, a catechism that seems to have been put into use immediately, although we find no newly published versions of it until 1545. Soon after he arrived, he similarly drafted a set of ecclesiastical ordinances for the city, creating a kind of church constitution, that was soon adopted by the city government and that contained provision for a new institution called the Consistory, designed to establish discipline. Within a few weeks this Consistory was meeting, once a week, on Thursdays. I understand that it continues to meet to this day, although admittedly with different personnel and functions.

It is to this Consistory that I want to draw particular attention. Calvin would not have returned to Geneva if the city had not agreed to create an institution of this kind. He threw himself into its activities with all his considerable energy. He attended its weekly meetings and participated in a major way in its activities. The Consistory's normal cases ended with either an admonition or a remonstrance, a kind of public scolding, delivered on behalf of the Consistory by one of the ministers who made up half of its membership but in most cases by Calvin himself. After his death, one of his biographers even said that Calvin administered all of these public scoldings. That is an exaggeration, but he clearly administered most of them. Some of the Consistory's more serious cases ended with a sentence of excommunication. Calvin insisted that a sentence of excommunication could be levied and lifted only by the Consistory, that it could not be appealed to the city government or overruled by the city's councils. When there was a possibility that this might happen, Calvin and his fellow ministers threatened to leave Geneva. After years of struggle, they won their way on this point. From then on, the administration of consistorial discipline became one of the most obvious and outstanding features of life in Reformed Geneva. The written registers of the sessions of this Consistory still survive, with only a few short gaps. Their manuscript originals are kept in the Archives d'Etat de Genève, and they are being made widely available in a critical edition by a team of scholars I have organized, published here in Geneva by the Librairie Droz.[1]

One of the things those registers make clear is the nature of discipline as established by Calvin. "Discipline" had a much broader meaning for Calvin than it has for many modern thinkers. To be sure, the Consistory inherited some of the functions of the pre-Reformation bishop's court. It was responsible for all cases involving the institution of marriage, beginning with the breach-of-promise cases most prominent in that court, adding suits for divorce,

1. *Registres du Consistoire de Genève au temps de Calvin*, ed. Thomas A. Lambert and Isabella M. Watt, with the assistance of Jeffrey R. Watt and M. Wallace McDonald, under the supervision of Robert M. Kingdon, in four volumes to date (Geneva: Droz, 1996, 2001, 2004, and 2007). A translation into English of volume 1 was published by Eerdmans in 2000.

including not only the separation of spouses permitted under Catholic canon law but including also, for the first time, divorce with permission to marry again. The Consistory also inherited some of the functions of regulating sexual morality that had been exercised before the Reformation by city courts. It no longer permitted prostitution under careful controls as had the earlier government. It tried to eliminate all forms of sexual activity outside of marriage.[2] These are the activities for which Geneva's Consistory is probably most widely remembered.

But the Consistory in actual fact went well beyond cases of this sort. A great deal of its time was devoted to resolving disputes—within families, as between parents and children or between brothers and sisters, among neighbors, and among business associates. It even developed special mechanisms for the resolution of these disputes, most commonly within Consistory meetings but sometimes leading to special ceremonies within church services, in which the parties to a dispute publicly forgave each other and promised to live together in peace in the future.[3]

In trying to resolve disputes over business, the Consistory also tried to challenge what it regarded as sharp practice. A number of times businessmen were called in and questioned about complicated deals involving loans of money and cloth that had to be paid back with materials of considerably greater value. These deals amounted to usury, since they permitted a rate of return on a loan well in excess of the rates permitted by city ordinances. Businessmen found guilty of these deals were subject to harsh penalties. So were people charged with other deviations from ethical business practice.[4]

The Consistory also tried to discover and suppress devotional practices regarded as "papist," leftovers from Roman Catholic times. A number of people were called in to say their prayers and then punished if they said them in Latin or included among them prayers for intercession addressed to the Virgin Mary or to the saints. Others were questioned about using rosaries, buying votive candles, fasting during Lent, and other Catholic devotional practices. Cases of this type were most common in the early years of the Consistory's operation and more often than not involved women rather than men, including many elderly women, some of them no doubt illiterate. People faced

2. See Robert M. Kingdon, *Adultery and Divorce in Calvin's Geneva* (Cambridge, MA: Harvard University Press, 1995), for its work in cases of this type.

3. Christian Grosse of the University of Geneva is beginning a massive study of the use of the Consistory and similar institutions throughout the French-speaking parts of Switzerland in conflict resolution during the early modern period.

4. See Mark Valeri, "Religion, Discipline, and the Economy in Calvin's Geneva," *Sixteenth Century Journal* 28, no. 1 (1997): 123–42, for more on these cases.

with accusations of this type who were willing to accept correction were usually treated fairly gently. Those who were stubborn could be treated harshly.[5]

The Consistory also handled many cases revealing a lack of respect for authority, both the authority of the city government and the authority of the city's pastors. And it handled a number of cases of behavior regarded as improper, such as dancing felt to be lascivious at wedding parties, or public drunkenness.

Controlling all these types of misbehavior is what the Consistory meant by discipline, and by the end of Calvin's ministry the Consistory had become remarkably successful in establishing it. Most Genevans either accepted discipline or left the city. Visitors to Calvin's Geneva often commented on the exemplary way people behaved there. Perhaps the most famous of these comments is found in John Knox's letter to Mrs. Locke of 1556. He told her that he had found in Geneva "the most perfect school of Christ that ever was in the earth since the days of the Apostles. In other places, I confess Christ to be truly preached, but manners and religion to be so sincerely reformed, I have not yet seen in any other place."[6] Accordingly, churches in other parts of Europe that looked to Geneva for leadership generally tried to establish a Genevan type of discipline, guided by an institution resembling the Consistory. That was certainly true in Scotland, where kirk sessions behaved much like the Genevan Consistory. The French Reformed similarly created consistories charged with maintaining discipline within their communities, although this had to be limited in most areas to church members alone, since hostile local governments tended to prevent its application to non-Protestants. Similarly, Dutch Calvinists tried to create consistories with powers of discipline, again limited in extent by governments willing to tolerate non-Calvinists. Many of them could look across the border with Germany, however, to Emden, sometimes called the "Geneva of the North," whose Reformed Kirchenrat exercised many of the powers of the Consistory in Geneva.[7]

This commitment to discipline can be found summarized with lapidary precision in a number of brief statements of required belief, called "confessions" then and now. It can be found specifically in clauses within these confessions on the *notae*, or marks, of the true church. At a number of times in Christian

5. For more on these cases, see Thomas A. Lambert, "Preaching, Praying, and Policing the Reform in Sixteenth-Century Geneva," PhD diss., University of Wisconsin–Madison, 1998.

6. "John Knox to Mrs. Ann Locke, Geneva, 9 December 1556" in David Laing, ed., *The Works of John Knox* 4 (Edinburgh: J. Thin, 1895), 240–41.

7. See Heinz Schilling and Klaus-Dieter Schreiber, eds., *Die Kirchenratsprotokolle der Reformierten Gemeinde Emden, 1557–1620*, 2 vols. (Cologne, Vienna: Böhlau, 1989, 1992).

history when competing institutions have each claimed to be the only true church of Christ, these institutions have listed the marks by which a true church can be known. That happened again at the time of the Reformation. Roman Catholics generally insisted on a fairly long list of marks, including government by bishops who can trace descent from the apostles, the custody of miracles and prophetic light, doctrines as defined in a highly technical way, and so on. Lutherans, in their famous Confession of Augsburg first presented in 1530, insisted that there are only two marks of a true church: "The church is the assembly of saints in which the gospel is taught purely and the sacraments are administered rightly." All that is needed is correct teaching and proper sacraments. There is no requirement of good behavior. There is no necessary structure, charged, among other things, with regulating behavior.

This two-mark definition of the true church, however, did not satisfy all early Protestants. Like Luther's doctrine of justification by faith alone, it could lead to antinomianism, undermining all ethics. In fact, it did among some early Lutherans. There were Lutherans who were so violently opposed to Catholic doctrines of good works that they opposed good works in general. For example, Nikolaus von Amsdorf, one of Luther's earliest supporters, in 1559 published a polemical tract with the title *That the Proposition, "Good Works Are Detrimental to Salvation," Is a Correct, True Christian Proposition, Taught and Preached by Saint Paul and Luther.* These people clearly did not fully understand Luther's own argument that man is saved by "faith active in love."[8]

Among early Protestants who found this definition of the true church to be incomplete were a number of religious radicals, often called Anabaptists. They complained that communities being organized by Lutherans were full of hypocrites, and they needed to find some way of disciplining their members. They favored use of a "ban," of driving these hypocrites out of their communities and refusing to recognize them as Christians at all. A few early Lutherans reacted to this complaint by suggesting that Protestant communities should indeed support discipline and should publicize this decision by proclaiming discipline to be a third mark of the true church. One of the earliest of them was a theologian named Erasmus Sarcerius, who worked first in Reformed Nassau and then in Lutheran Leipzig and Mansfeld.[9] Another was Martin Bucer, the Reformer of Strasbourg, who had great influence all over southern Germany and, late in life, in England as well. Bucer, in fact, campaigned strenuously for

8. Here I quote the felicitous title of a book by George W. Forell.

9. See James C. Spalding, "Discipline as a Mark of the True Church in Its Sixteenth-Century Lutheran Context," in *Piety, Politics, and Ethics: Reformation Studies in Honor of George Wolfgang Forell*, ed. Carter Lindberg (Kirksville, MO: Sixteenth Century Journal Publishers, 1984), 119–38.

the creation of a disciplinary institution in Strasbourg but never succeeded. He may well have been reacting to criticism from a large community of Anabaptists in Strasbourg. The government of that city, however, did not want it. Toward the end of Bucer's career it permitted him to establish a series of voluntary "Christian fellowships," in which individuals agreed to submit themselves to the sort of discipline Bucer desired. But they were never mandatory and never established discipline over the entire community.[10]

Calvin lived in Strasbourg, from 1538 to 1541, while this struggle was going on, and he established close contacts with Bucer. In effect Calvin did in Geneva what Bucer wanted to do in Strasbourg. He found in Geneva a government more amenable to establishing social control of this type. That led to the establishment and eventual triumph of the Consistory.

Calvin never wrote this commitment into his theology. The passages in his *Institutes* describing the marks of a true church contain a formula that is basically Lutheran. And he did not insist on it in common statements of theological belief worked out with the Zwinglians, particularly in Zurich, designed to reveal to outsiders a common stand among Swiss Protestants. The Zurichers, now led by Henry Bullinger, were terribly afraid of the Anabaptists who had disrupted their program of reform, and they would thus have nothing to do with formulas that to them smacked of Anabaptism. They supported discipline, but they wanted it to be enforced by Christian governments. They did not want to entrust its application to ecclesiastical institutions like the Consistory. They would not give to the church a plenary power of excommunication. In the face of this disagreement, both Geneva and Zurich agreed to keep it to themselves, to avoid debating about it in public, to allow each group of cities to go its own way. That difference continued to fester, however, and broke out into the open after Calvin's death as the Erastian quarrel in the Palatinate. There the theologian Olevianus, in close touch with Geneva's Beza, pushed for discipline of a consistorial type, and the physician Erastus, in close touch with Zurich's Bullinger, opposed it. That quarrel led to similar arguments in England between Calvinist Puritans and Erastian Anglicans.

But the confessions adopted by churches outside of Switzerland that were purely Calvinist did add discipline as a necessary mark and thus advanced a three-mark definition of the true church. The first Scottish Confession of 1560, for example, includes an article on *notis* ("marks") by which the true church can be distinguished from the false. It says that there are three of them: "the trew preaching of the Word of God, . . . the right administration of the Sacraments of Christ Jesus . . . [and] Ecclesiastical Discipline uprightlie min-

10. See Amy Nelson Burnett, *The Yoke of Christ: Martin Bucer and Christian Discipline* (Kirksville, MO: Sixteenth Century Journal Publishers, 1994), esp. chap. 8.

istered." The Belgic Confession of 1561, summarizing the faith of the Dutch Reformed, includes a similar article, which reads in part: "The marks by which the true Church is known are these: if the pure doctrine of the gospel is preached therein; if she maintains the pure administration of the sacraments as instituted by Christ; if church discipline is exercised in the punishing of sin. . . . Hereby the true Church may certainly be known."

This commitment to discipline by early Calvinist churches strikes me as very important. It shows a fuller attention to what Calvin did in Geneva than to what he said. It also adopts a theological position that lays a fuller basis for ethics than the formulas preferred by Lutherans and Zwinglians. It merits more attention from theologians now engaged in ecumenical rapprochement. The failure to consider fully discipline as a mark of the true church in the relevant articles of several recent ecumenical statements is regrettable. The Leuenberg Agreement adopted by the Evangelical and Reformed churches of Germany in 1994, for example, in its clause 2.4.1 on "the classical marks of the church," sums them up as "the true proclamation of the gospel and the celebration of the sacraments in accordance with their institution." This is basically a Lutheran statement. It does concede, to be sure, in a subsequent clause on "further marks" (2.4.2) that "in the Reformed tradition" the mark of "church discipline" was added. The Formula of Agreement adopted by four churches of the Reformation in the United States in 1997, however, does not even go that far. Even though three of those churches, the Presbyterian Church (U.S.A.), the Reformed Church in America, and the United Church of Christ, are more Calvinist than Lutheran in their origins, they adopted the formula preferred within the fourth of those churches, the Evangelical Lutheran Church in America. Their formula states that these churches "recognize each other as churches in which the gospel is rightly preached and the sacraments rightly administered according to the word of God." There it stops. There is no mention at all of discipline.

To those interested in recovering Calvin's witness on social and economic life, I would like to commend consideration of discipline. I would like to bring to the attention of the modern Reformed community the importance of discipline as understood and exercised by John Calvin and make a plea for recognition of discipline in today's Reformed churches.

3

Calvin's View of Property

A Duty Rather Than a Right

François Dermange

The well-known thesis worked out by Max Weber on "the elective affinity between Calvinism and capitalism" in *The Protestant Ethic and the Spirit of Capitalism* (1905) has been so influential that we often see it as a fact that "Calvinism appears to be . . . closely related to the hard legalism and the active enterprise of bourgeois-capitalistic entrepreneurs."[1] To do so is to forget that Weber's thesis depends on debatable hypotheses: Is it true that Calvinism's fundamental dogma is predestination? Can we link Calvin, Calvinism, Puritanism, and Methodism in one and the same movement? Can we make the Reformer the father of what three centuries later a sociologist observes in a population that is only indirectly affected by his influence?

Rather than discussing Weber's thesis in detail, this essay intends to probe how close to each other Calvin and capitalism might be regarding the rights and duties of owners. For capitalists, the defense of property is fundamental. Owners must be able to enjoy their possessions in absolute security, in order to be encouraged to make their work more productive, to save, and to make commitments through contracts. For this purpose, the law protects property from envy, which unfailingly arises from countless desires and the scarceness of possessions. Most constitutions of modern democratic states thus regard as

I thank James C. G. Greig and Edward Dommen not only for their help in the translation of this paper, but also for their valuable comments.

1. Max Weber, *The Protestant Ethic and the Spirit of Capitalism*, trans. Talcott Parsons (London: Harper Collins Academic, 1991), 139.

fundamental rights the use (*usus*) of possessions, their exploitation (*fructus*), and their alienation (*abusus*), which are challenged by only a few rare exceptions in the interests of public order. Very frequently the defense of property is thought to be a natural law, which one readily relates to the divine will. The outline of this reasoning is in John Locke (1632–1704). Locke does of course recognize that God gave the earth to be shared by the whole of humanity, but he justifies the inequality in the distribution of property from its final cause: the preservation of all mankind as much as possible for the greater good of all.[2] Thus government, which has to aim at the common good,[3] has a clearly defined task: "Government has no other end but the preservation of property."[4] From this standpoint, forbidding theft is seen fundamentally in terms of the rights of the owner.

But, strikingly, Calvin gives this commandment a completely different meaning. First of all, he claims that Christians are subject to other standards than just the law, for the law sometimes recognizes ownership gained from fraud or violence. Christians for their part must hold strictly to the framework Christian "sincerity" imposes upon them:

> All the arts we use to enrich ourselves at the expense of others, when they depart from Christian sincerity which must be cherished above all else, leaving the proper path for some devious trickery or other form of harm, are to be regarded as thefts. Although those who behave in this way often win their case before the judge, yet God holds them to be none other than thieves.[5]

What does this actually mean? As we shall see in the interpretation of the eighth commandment ("You shall not steal") in the *Commentaries on the Four Last Books of Moses*, Calvin understands Christian sincerity as a complex dialectic between justice and love (*caritas/agape*).[6] The Christian owner must under-

2. John Locke, *Second Treatise of Civil Government*, ed. C. B. McPherson (Indianapolis: Hackett Publishing Co., 1980), §25, §182.

3. Ibid., §131, or the public good (§134), the good of society (§137), the good of the people (§138), and the good of mankind (§229).

4. Ibid., §94.

5. *Institutes of the Christian Religion* 2.8.45; ed. John T. McNeill, trans. Ford Lewis Battles (London: SCM Press, 1961), hereafter *Inst.* Most of the translations of Calvin quoted in this paper have been corrected by one of the editors of this volume.

6. *Commentaries on the Four Last Books of Moses, Arranged in the Form of a Harmony, by John Calvin; Transl. from the Original Latin, and Compared with the French Edition, with Annotations by Charles William Bingham* (Edinburgh: Printed for the Calvin Translation Society, 1852–1855), hereafter *O.T. Harmony*. This English translation follows the Latin edition published by Henry Stephanus in 1563 under the title *Mosis libri V, cum Johannis Calvini Commentariis, Genesis seorsum: reliqui quatuor in formam harmoniae digesti. Praeter indices duos alphabeticos rerum quarundam in hisce Johannis Calvini commentariis notabilium,*

stand the meaning of his duty in practical relations with God and his neighbor without getting out of it by appealing to some usefulness for society in his wealth. Still more astonishingly, the Reformer claims that this Christian interpretation of the commandment is not basically specific to Christians but has a universal political import. Of course, the requirement for love is not so clear when we move away from the reference to the Mosaic law, but from this it does not remain less true that all human beings know in their conscience that they have a duty not to do harm to others and to support them through the possessions entrusted to them.

Before looking more closely at the Reformer's position, it is right to spend a few words recalling how he understood what the law implies. Here Calvin is in line with Luther's thinking on the uses of the law, which he extends by modifying it.[7] For Luther, the law, spiritually, has only a negative function—namely, to make us disillusioned about ourselves by confronting us with the ideal of the divine will. It is there only to make us see our sin and turn us toward the grace we freely receive in Christ. Justified believers then no longer have need of the law, because through the reception of the Holy Spirit they act from then onward *hilariter et sponte*—spontaneously and with joy. The sole positive dimension of the law is political: to establish a secular order of constraint that can curb evildoers so that the gospel may be peacefully proclaimed.

The first change of emphasis introduced by Calvin consists in setting the *abrogatory* or *elenchtic* use of the law in the context of teaching about the covenant: while it is necessary to awaken apathetic spirits and break down their arrogance by confronting them with the holiness of God, fear in itself does not have the final say. The grace by which God responds to it takes the form of a mutual commitment: God adopts the believer as his child, and the latter undertakes to respect the will of God. The law then takes on a central spiritual position, as through it the covenant is sealed. As opposed to Luther, Calvin does not think that the New Covenant sets aside that function of the law, as by contrast the enlivening Spirit given to believers bestows on them the power that the Jews lack, namely, to fulfill the requirements of the will of God.[8] The law covers every field of life and guides believers toward their sanctification. Thus, Calvin can highlight a new use of the law, which he calls didactic or educational and which he values as the main one. Through a process Calvin calls

---

calci huius voluminis adjectos, unum in Genesin, alterum in reliquos quatuor libros in formam harmoniae dispositos: habes et tertium, qui, singulorum capitum quilibet versus (variè alioqui, prout operis ratio postulavit, dispersi) quota pagina inveniri possint, protinus indicabit. Calvin himself executed the French translation published the next year by François Estienne.

7. The term "uses of the law" (*usus legis*) appears between 1531 and 1535 in Luther's revision of his *Commentary on Galatians*.

8. *Inst.* 2.7.6–12. Cf. Eric Fuchs, *La morale selon Calvin* (Paris: Cerf, 1986), 49–56.

"synecdoche," each commandment is then displayed in all its depth.[9] Even when it is stated negatively ("Thou shalt not"), one can only grasp its scope by giving a positive turn to it. Not killing is not enough if we are to fulfill our obligation toward others, but "we are to aid our neighbour's life by every means in our power."[10] Interpreting the law by love makes unlimited demands on the latter, undermining a justice that is made captive to the logic of *do ut des*. While justice enjoins respect for the limits of the things forbidden by norms that are fundamentally negative,[11] love requires giving others priority in charity.[12]

Economic relations are not exempted from this approach. Those who have experienced conversion, gratuitous justification by grace through faith, and the call for sanctification have a different way of looking at their relation toward others and their possessions. Thus, where the question relates to the economy, it is first of all in relation to God and is somewhat negative in tone: economic activity must not obscure the place that is properly God's, and the Sabbath is necessary to arrange for a period of rest, which is for communicating with God. Thus, economic ethics is measured in terms of the first "table"—"You shall have no other gods before me," the first commandment, and "Remember the Sabbath day, and keep it holy," the fourth commandment.[13] This unmasks the childish arrogance of wanting to save one's life by accumulating goods, forgetting that safety depends only on the sovereign God.[14] Economic ethics bring in the relation to one's neighbor only as a second step. The transition is made through the indirect, "incidental" consequences of the precepts of the first table: "By means of the Sabbath the family and the cattle shall be benefited" by a day of rest,[15] and

9. Generally, the principle of synecdoche takes the whole for the part. See *Commentary on a Harmony of the Evangelists, Matthew, Mark and Luke; Transl. from the Original Latin and Collated with the Author's French Version by William Pringle* (Edinburgh: Printed for the Calvin Translation Society, 1845), 2:396. Hereafter this work will be cited as *N.T. Harmony*.

10. *Inst.* 2.8.9.

11. *Sermons on Deuteronomy*, Deut. 19:14–15; in *Calvini opera, Corpus Reformatorum*, ed. G. Baum, E. Cunitz, E. Reuss (Brunswick: Schwetschke, 1871), 27:568–69.

12. Cf. *Inst.* 3.3.16.

13. The Decalogue is traditionally divided into two "tables," the first (the four first commandments) dealing with our relationship to God and the second with our relationships with neighbors.

14. See André Biéler, *Calvin's Economic and Social Thought* (Geneva: World Alliance of Reformed Churches and World Council of Churches, 2005) and the quotations from Calvin he gives in it to prove the dangers of wealth, a naive attempt to escape from God by giving oneself over to a form of idol-worship that in the end only enslaves (278–79).

15. *O.T. Harmony* 2:438, on Exod. 23:12. In this passage on the fourth commandment, the incidental use of the Sabbath is again referred to. The French version is more precise, stating that "l'utilité est accidentale," which is referring to the scholastic dialectic of "accident" (*Commentaires de M. Jean Calvin sur les cinq livres de Moïse* [Harmonie] [Geneva: François Estienne, 1564], 368).

as Calvin comments on it, following Deuteronomy, honoring God is on the same level as the equity that is extended to foreign servants and slaves.[16] Even if the second table is thus secondary in relation to the requirement of serving and worshiping God, through it a genuine examination of each person can be made, verifying their practical commitment to showing God their gratitude.[17] The principle of synecdoche is then applicable to the eighth commandment; beyond forbidding theft, the believer must provide for the needs of those who are in distress:

> What is said in God's Law? You shall not steal. There you have it in a single word. But the purpose of the lawgiver must be noted . . . that if we do not provide for our neighbours as best we can, God will condemn us and regard us as thieves.[18]

The second corrective introduced by Calvin relates to the political use of the law. Far from giving it just the one function of constraining the wicked, Calvin sees in this a sign of Providence's commitment to sustaining a truly human life, independently of the bounds of the church. Through the norms Providence has in a natural way made known to everyone in his or her conscience, God bears witness to his will to preserve humanity through an order that will enable everyone to live a decent life.

THE RELIGIOUS INTERPRETATION OF THE EIGHTH COMMANDMENT

With these great principles laid down, let us come to the commentary on the eighth commandment on the basis of the Decalogue and various other texts Calvin associates with it. We shall not be surprised that the commentary is explicitly divided between the spiritual meaning for the attention of Christians and its "underlying political elements" beyond the bounds of the church.

Let us begin with the former. The introductory explanation states straightaway that the purpose of the law is given only in relation to charity:

> Since charity is the end of the Law, we must seek the definition of theft from thence. This, then, is the rule of charity, that every one should keep peacefully what belongs to him and have the enjoyment of it, and that no one should do to another what he would not have done to himself.[19]

16. *O.T. Harmony*, 2:438, on Exod. 20:10.
17. *N.T. Harmony*, 2:396, on Matt. 19:18.
18. *Sermons on Deuteronomy*, Deut. 22:1–4; in *Calvini opera*, 28:10.
19. *O.T. Harmony*, 3:110, on Exod. 20:15.

By a strikingly concise comment, Calvin thus straightaway short-circuits the charity and justice that are given formal treatment in the Golden Rule, "Do not do to others what you would not want to be done to yourself."[20] The principles of the Golden Rule are equality and reciprocity, which are the mark of every conception of justice. By seeing themselves as just like others and applying to themselves the principles they expect others to follow toward them, Christians are not only *just* but also *charitable*. For charity in this initial approach is defined less by the specific standards of justice (Calvin states in contrast to these that "the philosophers deliver nearly the same doctrine")[21] than by practical concern. To be charitable is to behave in an upright and honest way, in accordance with standards that everyone knows.

But is this not to suggest that it is sufficient to abstain from doing harm to others in order to meet one's obligations to them? This is why Calvin hastens to remind us of the principle of synecdoche: "an affirmative precept, as it is called, is connected with the prohibition."[22] Charity is not content with respecting standards: it knows that behind these, actual people are always at stake:

> God . . . has laid mankind under mutual obligation to each other, that they may seek to benefit, care for, and succour each other. . . . We must endeavour, as far as possible, that every one should safely keep what he possesses, and that our neighbour's advantage should be promoted no less than our own.[23]

In this second sense, charity has not broken with justice, as we again find in it the principles of equality and reciprocity that are characteristic of it ("mutual obligation to each other," "our neighbour's advantage no less than our own"), but this time, the Golden Rule takes on a positive form, as in the gospel: "In everything do to others as you would have them do to you; for this is the law and the prophets" (Matt. 7:12; cf. Luke 6:31). This second way of stating the idea changes the meaning of the law itself. Mutuality is not restricted to the logic of contracts and of the mutual obligations of equals. It is a mutuality of service.

More specifically, the commentary on Leviticus 19:11, which follows, enables Calvin to illustrate his thesis. Believers must not only "deal sincerely, in good faith and honestly with each other," without deception or violence, but also behave humanely. Calvin illustrates this by the example of relations

20. In its negative form the Golden Rule is found in the LXX (Tobias 4:15 and Ecclesiasticus 31/34:15), and in a variant in Acts 15:20, 29 (in the *Codex Bezae* [D]). Attributed to Hillel, it is also quoted in Rabbinic Judaism (*Shabbath* 31a [Talmud Babli]) where it is also described as "the whole of the Torah, the rest being commentary."

21. *O.T. Harmony*, 3:111, on Exod. 20:15.

22. Ibid.

23. Ibid.

between employer and worker. Of course, the employer must fulfill his or her obligations, but not without regard to the timing; the poor person who has only his work as the source of his livelihood must receive his wages before the end of the evening. Here we are clearly on the level of contractual relations (the wage represents the equivalent of the work provided), but concern for persons commits the employer to more than mere respect for his strict obligations in the way he fulfills them. Following the example through, the commentary on Deuteronomy 24:14–15 goes a step further. The exchange must not simply take into account the services rendered and their reciprocal but also the fact that the wealthy and the poor are not in an equal situation. The sole wealth of the poor person lies in the work of his hands. Paying heed to the time limit for paying the worker is no longer enough if the wage he or she receives is not enough to live on. Another logic then places itself above that of the contract. The daily work of the poor must enable them to live:

> Humanity is recommended to us in general lest, while the poor labour at our service, we should arrogantly abuse them as if they were our slaves, or should be illiberal and stingy towards them, since nothing can be more unjust than that, when they have served us, they should not at least have enough to live upon frugally.[24]

Even though Calvin does not quote it directly, he is certainly thinking of the parable of the Laborers in the Vineyard (Matt. 20: 1–16). An employer enters into a contract with some unemployed people and at the same time settles on the hours of work to be provided and the wages to be received at the end of the day—a denarius. But then as the day goes on, the employer hires in turn other workers with whom he makes no agreement. When the evening comes and he goes to pay each of them, beginning with those who came last, he gives them a denarius. He then gives the same amount to the others. Those who had worked since the morning are angry: "These last worked only one hour, and you have made them equal to us who have borne the burden of the day and the scorching heat." Then the employer answers them thus: You have received what you were owed. We had agreed on one denarius, and that you have. But I must also give that amount to these last, "because I am good." Thus, we can see what is meant by juxtaposing the kingdom of God and the economic world: the two worlds overlap without denying each other. Nothing in the parable challenges the logic of the contract, the equivalence of the things exchanged or the difference between employer and worker, and so on. But Jesus links this with another logic: that in which the unemployed are first and foremost persons who must be able to stay alive quite apart from their output or the needs

24. *O.T. Harmony*, 3:114, on Deut. 24:14–15.

of the economy. In this way Matthew separates two levels of the relation to money, which complement each other and are not mutually contradictory: an economic level that follows its own rules, and the kingdom of God in which money serves a purpose, which is to enable everyone to have a life.

Calvin follows the same idea. Without challenging equality and reciprocity as the matrix for justice, he stresses that justice goes beyond the strict framework of contractual relations: the rich have specific obligations toward the poor *because* they are poor, and an employer who does not provide for his workers is a tyrant, even if no contractual or legal obligation compels him to do so.[25]

In this way Calvin explicitly distinguishes this religious interpretation of justice from legal and political justice. God summons consciences to appear before his judgment seat, not before an earthly judge, and hence one must say that this law is "spiritual."[26] So then, does this mean we have departed from the actual locus for justice? Not for Calvin, if one can clearly see that the virtue of liberality crosses the line between equity and charity, setting its seal on the continuity between the one and the other. We shall return to this.

The sum is that we should liberally and freely give everyone what is equitable.[27] Having clearly expounded the meaning of justice, Calvin completes his analysis of the eighth commandment with the commentary on some other passages that sharpen up the sense. As I have said, justice must not ignore the actual situation of individuals, but for all that, it must not confine itself to one's own narrow circle. The Golden Rule must apply "towards all without exception"[28] and especially toward foreigners:

> God commands [us] to love strangers and foreigners as themselves. Hence it appears that the name of neighbour is not confined to our kindred, to people who live near us or other familiars, but extends to the whole human race.[29]

If an owner opens his eyes he will—like the Samaritan (Luke 10:30), whom Calvin then mentions—find occasions for exhibiting that "other principle of equity," which is compassion.[30] For example, where repayment of debts is the

25. Ibid.

26. Ibid.

27. *O.T. Harmony*, 3:115, on Deut. 25:4. I follow closely the French text (*Commentaires de Moïse*; Harmonie, 424). The Bingham English version is less explicit: "The sum is that we should freely and voluntarily pay what is right." Sometimes the Latin version is more precise than the French; for example, instead of "disposed to such liberality," the French says only *pitoyable* (pitiful, deplorable, dismal) (*O.T. Harmony*, 3:124, on Deut. 24:10; *Commentaires de Moïse*; Harmonie, 427).

28. *O.T. Harmony*, 3:116, on Lev. 19:33–34.

29. Ibid.

30. *O.T. Harmony*, 3:122, on Deut. 24:6.

question, justice cannot restrict itself to the simple terms of the contract, as a contract may be a cover for getting the upper hand. Thus, justice has to see to it that a loan will at least serve the purpose for which it is given: to facilitate exchange. Even if the debtor is insolvent, there would be an injustice in demanding repayment of a loan by mortgaging the chance for the poor person to continue carrying on his business. Therefore, the creditor must not be seen to be "too rigorous" or "iron-hearted" by depriving the poor of "what they need to earn their living and provide for themselves," their tools, their clothes, or their bed.[31]

In one sense, the argument is still set in the matrix of reciprocity, for the wealthy can expect a return through the prayer of the poor person who will gain for him divine favor:

> Although the poor have not the means of repaying us in this world for the good which we do for them, still they have the power of recompensing us before God, i.e., by obtaining favour for us through their prayers.[32]

But this accountant's logic does not hold the whole way through. When charity is at its highest level, the qualities of the poor person are no longer what prompt the gift. Those who take Christ as their model and let themselves be moved by compassion come into the logic of the love of the gospel, which gives when actually not knowing of a possible recompense:

> This is, in point of fact, the genuine trial of our charity, when, in accordance with Jesus Christ's precept, we lend to those of whom we expect no return (Luke 6:35). . . . Hence he proposes another sort of liberality, which is plainly gratuitous, in giving assistance to the poor, not only because one puts the principal at risk, but *because* they do not have the means to make a return in kind.[33]

Through these different approaches to the eighth commandment—twin interpretations of the Golden Rule, practical concern for others, universal application, and compassion—the Christian meaning of the norm emerges, ascending gradually away from the justice of *do ut des* and toward love, a love which is above all spontaneous and free of any ulterior motive. But where does it display less motivation than when it is directed toward those whose behavior ought rather to call for the opposite approach? Just as God's love is love for sinners, so too Christian love is love for those who do not merit it:

31. Ibid.
32. *O.T. Harmony*, 3:124, on Deut. 24:10.
33. *O.T. Harmony*, 3:126–27, on Exod. 22:25; my italics.

> The sum therefore is, that the faithful should be kind and human by being kind to everyone, that they may imitate their heavenly Father, and should not only tend to the good who are worthy of it, but should also treat with kindness those who have not deserved it.[34]

Calvin could have left matters there, but because charity involves practical caring, he strives to explain the practical consequences of the matrix on which he has just thrown light. Corresponding to the upward movement of justice from *do ut des* to love is the downward movement of love toward its practical application. Calvin then defends a fresh thesis: in this return movement, charity cannot be practiced directly. Even in a broadly "Christian" society, the social expression of love requires mediation operating through the norms of reciprocity—and therefore through justice.

Calvin outlines the method for this in his commentary on Exodus regarding the rules for usury. Drawing on Moses' work as the standard, he reckons that faithfulness to the biblical text cannot consist in directly transferring Old Testament standards into a society that no longer has anything in common with ancient Judaism. It is better to come back to the heart of what religion requires—charity—and to endeavor to give an interpretation of this that respects what it means in a decidedly new situation, even by setting norms seemingly contrary to the biblical text.[35]

> The judicial law, however, which God prescribed to His ancient people, is only so far abrogated as that what charity dictates should remain, *i.e.*, that our brethren, who need our assistance, are not to be treated harshly.[36]

While preserving the appropriate teleology for religious ethics—"Nor had God any other object in view, except that mutual and brotherly affection should prevail"[37]— Calvin interprets it by taking into account the different status between ancient Judaism and the Christian church. Whereas ancient Judaism was a relatively closed, homogeneous society in the midst of pagan culture, Christianity is spread among every society. But while prohibiting lending at interest among Jews, Moses did see that it was necessary to allow it in trading with non-Jews for a simple reason: if usury were also forbidden in relation to pagan peoples, the Jews would be placed at a disadvantage, because they would have to pay interest that their Gentile debtors would not be obliged

34. *O.T. Harmony*, 3:134, on Exod. 23:4.
35. Here Calvin's thinking is parallel to the distinction on the political level between equity and legal enactments (*Inst.* 4.20.16).
36. *O.T. Harmony*, 3:128, on Exod. 22:25.
37. Ibid.

to pay. If there is not "a just reciprocity," then "one party must needs be injured."[38] In other words, charity operates only among equals, and among those not equal it is better first to reestablish justice in order not to risk being unjust with the excuse of being charitable. The Reformer concludes that "this is the only intercourse that can be endured: when the condition of both parties is similar and equal."[39] Since Christianity's domain is the "community of the human race" there can no longer be a question of prohibiting interest.[40] To highlight charity, one had to extend to relationships among Christians the principle that, in the time of Moses, was only valid in the relationship between Jews and pagans. The only way of "sparing all without exception" is to ensure mutuality through reciprocity in such a fashion that Christians maintain a like equity towards all.[41] The downward movement of love toward social ethics thus goes beyond the Golden Rule—"the universal rule of justice, and especially from the declaration of Jesus Christ, on which hang the law and the prophets: *Do not unto others what ye would not have done to thyself* (Matthew 7:12),"[42] without the need to invoke a natural law inspired by Plato or Aristotle (as does contemporary Roman Catholic ethics).[43] The Reformer concludes that nothing is to be condemned a priori, but "the law of equity will better prescribe than any lengthy discussions."[44]

Calvin again reminds us that charity does not dispense with justice. His purpose is to condemn judges who want to "depart from equity in favour of the poor," in the name of the gospel, and "follow out a foolish idea of mercy" by favoring the poor.[45] In the name of justice, there should not be any question of providing for the needs of the destitute by causing harm to the wealthy.[46] The Reformer agrees with Paul: while the wealthy have a duty to give alms, one must not compel them to share their possessions.[47] Whatever may be the merit of charity, and the concern to free the poor from tyranny, one should not become less upright by even a hair's breadth.[48]

38. Ibid.
39. Ibid.
40. Ibid., here, according to the French version (*Commentaires de Moïse*; Harmonie, 429).
41. Ibid.
42. *O.T. Harmony*, 3:129, on Exod. 22:25.
43. Ibid., 3:131.
44. Ibid.
45. "Pour suivre une folle miséricorde" (*O.T. Harmony*, 3:138, on Exod. 23:6). The precision is only in the French text (*Commentaires de Moïse*; Harmonie, 443).
46. "God does not indeed require that those who have abundance should so profusely give away their produce, as to despoil themselves by enriching others" (*O.T. Harmony*, 3:152, on Deut. 24:19–22).
47. *O.T. Harmony*, 3:151–52, on Deut. 24:19–22; cf. *N.T. Harmony*, 1:333, on Matt. 6:19.
48. Ibid.

We can now describe the religious ethic of the eighth commandment under three headings: (1) If they are not to be thieves, Christians must not only respect the rights of others but must "not permit the poor who have no means of support to be trampled on."[49] (2) Calvin takes great care not to set against each other the different gradations he has defined, by keeping for charity only its most selfless forms. In a sense, all of them express something both of justice and of charity. (3) Calvin will have shown the inescapable dialectic between the gospel's love and the Golden Rule. Justice and charity require reciprocity but also, in the name of compassion, positive humane actions, or gifts *going in one direction only*. Love asks more of justice than the Golden Rule. But, conversely, love could not set aside the force of justice in the name of compassion's radical nature. One cannot have love *without* the Golden Rule.

THE POLITICAL CONSEQUENCES OF THE EIGHTH COMMANDMENT

The eighth commandment's Christian ethic thus calls for justice and love being kept together without confusion or separation. But what of the political angle? The Reformer tackles this question in the succeeding part of his commentary, under the heading "The Political Consequences of the Eighth Commandment."[50]

That Calvin places himself in the secular domain on this occasion must not surprise us. Contrary to a notion that is too generally accepted, he was interested in natural law. He strongly opposes any direct relation between theology and politics. In particular, he is against authority being given to biblical norms to organize society, no matter how well attested these may be.[51] Why? Because the texts are not in themselves normative but are to a great extent dependent on the specific context that engendered them. Thus, we have to come back to the foundation under the biblical standards that these standards sought to interpret in a past situation. At the end of this critical work, Calvin claims that the only norms that retain their relevance are those of the "moral law," that is, the Decalogue.[52]

49. *Sermons on Deuteronomy*, on Deut. 5:19; in *Calvini opera*, 26:358.

50. Literally, "political dependences of the eighth commandment." "Dependences" is vague in English, and the standard English translation is "Political supplements to the eighth commandment" (*O.T. Harmony*, 3:140), but this is not clear as a rendering of the French word *dépendances*. *Dépendances* has wide connotations, but the main idea is that the political rules are under control of the eighth commandment.

51. *Inst.* 4.20.16.

52. *O.T. Harmony*, preface, 1:xvi; cf. *Inst.* 4.20.14, 16.

To this Calvin adds another thesis: if the law of Moses as a whole relates to the Decalogue, paradoxically there is no need of Moses in order to grasp its meaning, for Providence is not dumb. It takes care of human beings, not only through the rules of nature, or by guiding them without their realizing it, like inanimate beings or animals. The first way it acts is to impart to human beings the rules and institutions through which they can ensure a minimum of genuinely human life. Calvin, correlating this idea with Pauline remarks on natural law,[53] then maintains that the Gentiles through their consciences have access to a universal natural law that acts as a framework for political action. Because secular authorities naturally take the Decalogue as the rule, we can think that they are aiming at the good, as Romans 13 would have it.[54]

Calvin can interrelate these two theses with the idea that the natural law known to the Gentiles through their consciences is nothing other than the moral law he places at the heart of the revealed law, in other words, the Decalogue:

> Given that the law of God which we call moral, is nothing else than the testimony of natural law, and of that conscience which God has engraved in the hearts of all people, it is evident the whole of this equity of which we now speak is prescribed in it. Hence it alone ought to be the aim, the rule, and the end of all laws. Wherever laws are formed after this rule, directed to this aim, and restricted within this bounds, they cannot be disapproved by us, however much they may differ from the law of Moses, or from each other.[55]

Calvin can then argue in favor of there being agreement between the revealed law and the different legal systems that prevailed among the Gentiles,[56] for the Decalogue is at the point where two logics intersect: that of Providence, which ensures that the world will endure, and that of the revealed God who sets his seal on the covenant through his Law.[57] Thus, the political and religious spheres hold together, not only on the higher level in their respective relations to the sovereignty of God but also on the lower level, by reference to a law

53. Paul does mention the Gentiles' natural knowledge of the law in Romans 2:14–15 only to establish their lack of excuse. With this denunciatory use of natural law, Calvin links a positive use of it which Providence also desires. See, e.g., *Sermons on Deuteronomy*, on Deut. 19:14–15, in *Calvini opera*, 27:568–69.

54. *Commentary upon the Acts of the Apostles; Ed. from the original English Transl. of Christopher Fetherstone by Henry Beveridge* (Edinburgh: Printed for the Calvin Translation Society, 1844), 262–63, on Acts 25:11.

55. *Inst.* 4.20.16.

56. *Sermons on Deuteronomy*, on Deut. 19:14–15, in *Calvini opera*, 27:568–69.

57. The Decalogue has been there from the beginning. It is because of the "perversity of our nature" that God had to reveal it to Moses and to provide through his providence for political institutions and this world's means of enforcing law and order (*Sermons on Deuteronomy*, on Deut. 16:18–19, in *Calvini opera*, 27:409.

common to them. Religious and political personalities do indeed have different views of that law: the one group sees it as a set of negative standards that the others turn into positive obligations in the service of other people, in terms of a perfectionist ethic of virtues. Likewise, the natural understanding of the law is not at all enough in the eyes of believers, for it is unaware of the more essential element in the first table: to put our trust in God, to call upon his name or keep his Sabbath.[58] But beyond this difference in interpretation, the principle is clear: through the dispositions of Providence and the resources of natural understanding, the Decalogue provides the basis for legitimizing politics and indicates its bounds. The magistrate extends the witness of conscience before "the judgment seat of God" when this naturally reveals what the Decalogue contains. His task is to establish a common life in a social context in accordance with the rules discovered by each person within himself or herself.[59]

So what of economics? Related to the purpose of Providence, it has to be of service to the life of all human beings, and exchange is held to be necessary in relation to this condition, for "when one can no longer buy or sell, human society has so to speak disappeared."[60] If Calvin maintains that the law must protect property or contracts, the reason is that trade serves the economic purpose of providing for human beings in friendship and peace.[61] It even has to be said that economics has a fiduciary dimension.[62] Everyone must be able to have confidence in the weights, measures, currency, and all common "rules of the game."[63] The positive nature of economics also goes hand in hand with recognizing property and contracts, but therefore neither does the law on property nor the protection of contracts have absolute value; they are relative to communication among human beings and to justice.[64]

We still have to determine how these universal rules are to be guaranteed—certainly by a conscientious awareness that God summons us to his judgment seat—with promises and threats. But conscientious awareness is not enough, and hence the intervention of the civil magistrate is necessary.

"Political consequences" indicates that political interpretation springs from the law (it depends on it) but clearly belongs to the secular plane. Understood

58. *Inst.* 2.2.24; cf. 1.6.2.

59. *Inst.* 4.20.2.

60. *O.T. Harmony*, 3:20, on Lev. 19:35.

61. *O.T. Harmony*, 1:279, on Exod. 16:17.

62. *Commentaries on the Epistle of Paul the Apostle to the Romans; Transl. and Ed. by John Owen* (Edinburgh: Printed for the Calvin Translation Society, 1849), 98, on Rom. 2:15.

63. *Sermons on Deuteronomy*, on Deut. 19:14–15, in *Calvini opera*, 27:567; cf. Biéler, *Calvin's Economic and Social Thought*, 377–78.

64. *Sermons on Deuteronomy*, on Deut. 19:14, in *Calvini opera*, 27:567–68. Human beings have to "maintain mutual equity with each other," and to "follow and observe what is right" on "earthly affairs" (*O.T. Harmony*, 2:73, on Deut. 18:19). Cf. *Inst.* 4.20.9.

at the civil level, the consequences of the eighth commandment are limited to establishing a general framework, the principle of which is "not so exact and perfect; since in their enactment God has relaxed his just severity in consideration of the people's hardness of heart,"[65] but the framework expresses no less the structure of the Decalogue. Law must therefore not become detached from its markers. Each time it does, it can only go astray.

> The pagan legislators borrowed what God had ordained for his people. Draco, indeed, had been more severe in the city of Athens, but his laws were abolished by the general opinion of all. Solon who later succeeded him made the law which the Romans followed in their twelve tables. . . . But whoever weighs all this up wisely finds that both Solon and the Roman law-makers spoiled everything by departing from the law of God.[66]

We can now return to Calvin's commentary on the political consequences of the eighth commandment. I shall not stop here on a lengthy discussion regarding the different penalties aimed at defining the scope of how they are to be assigned and rewarded. I will merely mention that the commentary on Leviticus 24:18–21 is Calvin's opportunity to stress that the law must first judge the facts and only then weigh up the responsibility, by taking into account intentions, will, the desire to harm, and blameworthiness. Of greatest interest to us is the conception of justice that the Reformer defends.

As I have already mentioned, on the political level, the eighth commandment is comprehended not only under the aegis of commutative justice—checking on the equality of the things exchanged—but also of the Golden Rule as negatively stated.[67] Thus everyone, whether a believer or not, can recognize that slavery is tyranny and God "prescribes no more than pagan philosophers did, word for word."[68]

But is it enough to abstain from enslaving and stealing from the poor in order to be just? Certainly not for the Reformer, who maintains that the dialectic of justice and charity holds good also on the political level, even if less clearly than for religious ethics.[69] Having thus stated in the specifically religious part of his

65. *O.T. Harmony*, 3:140, on Exod. 22:1–4.

66. Ibid.

67. *O.T. Harmony*, 3:111, on Exod. 20:15.

68. *O.T. Harmony*, 3:164, on Lev. 25:39–55; cf. Seneca, *De beneficiis*, 3:22.

69. "Thus far God has declared that he will avenge all iniquities and by summoning thieves to appear before him, he has threatened them with eternal death. Now follow the civil laws, in which there is no juridical perfection, because God has abandoned his rigour in order to meet the hardness of the people's hearts." (This translation is based on the French version and not from the existing standard translations of the *O.T. Harmony* (*Commentaires de Moïse*; Harmonie, 433–34, on Exod. 22:1–4).

commentary that humanity and compassion constitute part of justice to relieve the poor, Calvin goes on to say:

> Pagan authors saw this, but not so clearly, when they demonstrated that men are born for each other and so must have fellowship with each other to uphold the community of the human race. Wherefore, that we may not defraud our neighbours, and so be accounted thieves in God's sight, let us learn, according to our several means, to be benefactors of those who need our help.[70]

Even on the political level, equity is aimed at mutuality and calls for a certain degree of distributive justice. Recognition of the right to ownership and the protection of contracts are conditioned by humanitarian obligations, which must temper too strict an applicaton of the principle of reciprocity.[71] When Calvin deals with the "political consequences" of the eighth commandment, he follows out the same idea, particularly regarding the repayment of debts. Addressing creditors, he exhorts them to show their humanity and not be "too rigid in exacting our debts, especially if we have to do with the needy, who are bowed down by the burden of poverty."[72]

Why so? According to the commentary on Deuteronomy 24:19–22, the reason seems to be theological. If every proprietor is exhorted to exercise liberality, this is because the richness of the harvest comes not only from his work but also from God's bountifulness. The proprietor is thus invited to show his gratitude to God by extending his generosity toward those who depend on him: "His bounty is exercised before our eyes, it invites us to imitate Him; and it is a sign of ingratitude, inhumanely and meanly to withhold what springs from his blessing."[73] But is revelation needed in order to know that all we have comes from God? Probably for Calvin it is in conscience, before God's judgment seat, that each person recognizes that it is from a god—no matter here which one—that our work receives its fruit.

SUMMARY AND CONCLUSION

As I stated at the beginning, the Reformer is less interested in ensuring the safety of property against the envy of others or in showing its social usefulness than in defining the duties of the wealthy in relation to the poor. As a Chris-

70. *O.T. Harmony*, 3:126, on Exod. 22:25.
71. See *O.T. Harmony*, 3:154, on Deut. 15:1–11; 3:152, on Deut. 24:19–22; 3:162–67, on Lev. 25:39–55.
72. *O.T. Harmony*, 3:154, on Deut.15:1–11.
73. *O.T. Harmony*, 3:152, on Deut. 24:19–22.

tian, but also simply as a human being, each individual is obliged to put the Golden Rule into practice as stated both negatively and positively. Thus, economic ethics is placed under the aegis of justice but also of charity, whether the latter takes the Christian form of love or of distributive justice.

Some commentators then object to the confusion of justice and love;[74] others are pleased about it.[75] But as we have seen, Calvin does not confuse justice and love when he refuses to contrast them.[76] Rather, one must see a dialectical relation between the two of them: in the religious as in the political sphere, the mutuality of justice is liable without love to remain a captive to the logic of *do ut des*, and charity without the Golden Rule is liable to do violence to justice.

Is Calvin misrepresenting love? This is the thinking of those who consider that the logic of love is not compatible with that of reciprocity, the basic principle of all justice. Even if Calvin sometimes uses some ambiguous expressions,[77] to me it seems that he fully respects the radical meaning of love in the gospel:

> Christ affirms that we do nothing for the honour of God when, in lending or doing other kind offices, we look to the mutual reward. He thus draws a distinction between charity and carnal friendship. Profane people have no simple affection for each other, but only an expectation of profit: and thus, every person turns back on themselves that affection which they entertain for others, as Plato also judiciously observes. But it is gratuitous generosity that Christ demands from his people—zeal to aid the helpless, from whom they can expect nothing in return.[78]

But Calvin does not wish to oppose the "free liberality" that is God's[79] and human or secular understandings of charity, for at least two reasons: (1) there is no clear break between liberality and impartiality, and (2) love can only be put into practice through the *lex caritatis*, which is the Golden Rule, with its principle of reciprocity.[80] The paradox is, moreover, not specific to Calvin, but is at the heart of the Lukan presentation of the Sermon on the Plain. Luke really hesitates to relate the Golden Rule to pagan wisdom or to revelation[81] and deliberately places the Golden Rule in the same literary sequence as the

74. E.g., Paul Wernle, *Der evangelische Glaube nach den Hauptschriften des Reformatoren* (Tübingen: Mohr, 1920), 149.

75. E.g., Günter Gloede, *Theologia Naturalis bei Calvin* (Stuttgart: W. Kohlhammer, 1935), 173–78.

76. As against Edward Dowey's claim in *The Knowledge of God in Calvin's Theology* (New York: Columbia University Press, 1952), 230.

77. *O.T. Harmony*, 3:124, on Deut. 24:10.

78. *N.T. Harmony*, 1:302, on Matt. 5:42 and Luke 6:34–35.

79. *O.T. Harmony*, 1:362, on Deut. 6:20.

80. *N.T. Harmony*, 1:304, on Matt. 5:43–44.

81. As opposed to Matthew, who sees in the Golden Rule a synthesis of Old Testament teaching (Matt. 7:12). Luke sees it as an expression of pagan wisdom (Luke 6:31).

love of one's enemies, which seems to contradict it.[82] However much the radical nature of the gospel may find fault with the justice of the Golden Rule for its concealed utilitarianism, it does not oppose this, because it needs it in order to acquire a practical shape.

Does Calvin misrepresent justice? This is what those people think who reproach him for having adulterated equity with elements that would not be comprehensible outside Christianity.[83] Perhaps Calvin in reality was more stamped with the ancient philosophical tradition than it seems. The different meanings he gives to equity are already present in Aristotle, especially the idea of liberality or indulgence.[84] When Calvin expresses equity in terms of the Golden Rule and opens up justice to positive obligations toward actual individuals, he is not betraying the best of humanism's legacy.

Liberality makes the transition between love and justice, showing that here again Calvin is rejecting the scholastic tradition less than is often thought: "Liberality is a part of righteousness, so that he must be deservedly held to be unrighteous who does not provide for the necessities of his brethren when he can."[85] For Calvin as for Aristotle, liberality is a necessary, subordinate extension of justice.[86] This is as much as to say that liberality is not necessarily a religious idea. It is in relation to justice that liberality is held to be a virtue.[87] By committing themselves to helping others, liberally minded persons seem to give more than what they are obliged in strict justice to do, but in this way they are only aiming at the equality that is at the heart of justice, restoring to each person his or her proper place.[88] But liberality is already pointing toward love, as Thomas Aquinas well understood.[89]

82. See Luke 6:31. Paul Ricoeur stresses this point to notable effect; see "The Golden Rule: Exegetical and Theological Perplexities," *New Testament Studies* 36 (1990): 392–97.

83. One might gather this from Guenther Haas, *The Concept of Equity in Calvin's Ethics* (Carlisle, England: Paternoster Press, 1997), which identifies several meanings for equity, only some of which are taken from the philosophical tradition of the ancient world. In particular, the idea of equity calling for a softened interpretation of law would be entirely owed to the scriptural tradition.

84. In the *Nicomachean Ethics*, *epieikeia* corrects the general nature of positive law (5:14.1137b), but in *Rhetoric*, it reminds us of both natural law (1.13.1–2, 13) and the indulgence/leniency that the judge has to demonstrate (1.93.17–19). Cf. Irena Backus, *Historical Method and Confessional Identity in the Era of the Reformation (1378–1615)* (Leiden: Brill, 2003), 66n9.

85. *O.T. Harmony*, 3:126, on Exod. 22:25.

86. Aristotle, *Nicomachean Ethics*, 4.1119b, 20s.

87. Aristotle, *Rhetoric*, 1.9.6, 1366b5.

88. Aristotle, *Nicomachean Ethics*, 4.1.1120b2, 1120a15.

89. Thomas Aquinas, *Summa theologica*, 2-2, q.80, 117, a.5, s.3; 2-2, q.80, 117, a.6, s.1; 2-2, q.31 a.1, s.2.

Thus, in relation to the eighth commandment Calvin strives to reconcile humanism and Christianity without toning down the features specific to each. His proposed model is poles apart from the concerns of dawning capitalism, of its defense of property and praise for the utilitarian benefits of amassing of wealth in the hands of a few. The ethic of property is more concerned with the duties of the wealthy than with their rights. Do his words nevertheless run counter to Weber's perceptions? Perhaps not, even if only indirectly. For if it is true that wealth first of all gives one obligations toward others, those who know they are stewards of possessions that do not belong to them will be inclined not to spend on themselves in pointless self-indulgence; they will invest the capital they have amassed in industries that will create jobs. Finally, it is possible that Reformed language about the responsibility of the wealthy paradoxically turned out to have an affinity with capitalism, but with a fundamental difference: its sole concern was to improve the actual situation of the poor, not in some hypothetical future, but by listening to those who today are weeping in silence.

4

Calvin and the Environment

Calvin's Views Examined through the Prism of Present-Day Concerns, and Especially of Sustainable Development

Edward Dommen

So this is a general rule that we must note well. Whenever we are encouraged to do damage or harm, let us remember that our Lord has provided lodging for us all in this world; he has provided us with the things he knows to be useful for our lives. If now I seek to despoil the land of what God has given it to sustain human beings, then I am seeking as much as I can to do away with God's goodness, which thus disappears. Am I worthy that the land sustain me, if in this way I want to do away with God's grace—which was as much for my neighbors as for me? Do I no longer want his grace to have currency and to reign? And am I not as it were as monster? There, I say, is what must firmly restrain us when we are driven by some mischief and poisoned so far as to damage trees and houses and similar things. Let us be restrained, realizing whom we are actually waging war against. It is not against the creatures but against the one who shows us here a reflection of his goodness, not only towards only one individual, but towards all, and we are included in that number.

But be that as it may[,] . . . if there is one thing we must do, it is to do no damage, as we know our Lord ordained the land to be as it were our nursing mother, and when it thus opens its entrails to

> sustain us, we should know that this is just as if God extended his hand to us and handed us proofs of his goodness.[1]

The foundations of Calvin's arguments concerning the environment (or nature or the creation—they were not distinct concepts in his day) are at root very simple:

1. God created all things for the benefit of humanity;
2. God created humanity to glorify him.

This essay will unpack that argument in order to bring out some of its particularly pregnant features in relation to the present-day debate on the environment and sustainable development.

GOD CREATED NATURE FOR HUMANITY

This point, which can be found in the epigraph, is made even more emphatically elsewhere in Calvin's works:

> In every respect, let us consider what God has done in heaven and on earth, it is all for our use and benefit. When he created the sun it was not to give himself light, but so that we should have light. Similarly with the moon and the stars: they are ordained to serve us. . . . In the same way, though the earth produces forage for the dumb animals, everything is in conformity with human needs, and in a word God wants us to recognize his fatherly goodness and the love he exerts towards us.[2]

> We know that it was chiefly for the sake of humankind that the world was made.[3] People are the most honorable and precious ornament of the earth. . . . For to what end are such a variety of fruits produced, and in such abundance, and are there so many enjoyable places, unless it be for the use and convenience of humanity?[4]

> In the very sequence of creation one better perceives God's paternal solicitude for man, since before forming him he prepares the world for

1. Sermon 119 on Deut. 20:16–20. Most of the passages from Calvin quoted in this essay are found in André Biéler, *La pensée économique et sociale de Calvin* (Geneva: Georg, 1961). Translations are my own and are not always identical to those in André Biéler, *Calvin's Economic and Social Thought* (Geneva: World Alliance of Reformed Churches and World Council of Churches, 2005).

2. Sermon 142 on Deut. 25:1–4.

3. *Institutes* (1560), 1.16.6.

4. Commentary on Ps. 24:1. The verse in question actually makes the converse point, which I take up in the next section.

> him and furnishes it with everything needed, indeed with an infinite abundance of all riches.[5]

The passage just quoted ends with a magnificent declaration: "Thus man was rich before he was born."

God Provides Generously

Calvin repeatedly insists that God not only provides for our needs but also for our pleasure and enjoyment. Calvin did not promote asceticism but rather a joyous sobriety with lucid generosity.[6]

> The Prophet wants it to be understood that God not only provides for men's necessity, and bestows upon them as much as is sufficient for the ordinary purposes of life, but that in his goodness he deals still more bountifully with them by cheering their hearts with wine and oil; for nature would certainly be satisfied with water to drink. It is true that it would be enough for human beings to have bread to keep them alive, but in a spirit of superabundance (as one says) God extends wine and oil in addition.[7]

In this setting Calvin denies the Malthusian bugbear which still haunts the environmental debate today: "It is impossible that there should be so great a multitude of people that the earth be incapable of supporting and nourishing them."[8]

In the present-day debate on the subject the fear that there will not be enough to go around is countered with two kinds of argument. The first is that "there is enough for everyone's need but not for everyone's greed," as Gandhi said. Calvin would not have formulated the argument in that way: we have just seen that he argued that God provides humanity with more than enough for their needs, that God even provides for their joys and pleasures. Nonetheless, as we shall see, he does insist for other reasons that we moderate our wants. The second argument is that the fruits of creation are badly distributed because we ignore our obligations to the poor. This will be examined later.

In 1987 the World Commission on Environment and Development formulated a particularly intricate definition of sustainable development (see the appendix). Often quoted, and even more often misquoted and truncated, it remains the reference against which the countless other definitions can be tested. In any event, the last element of the definition echoes Calvin's views:

5. Commentary on Gen. 1:26.

6. See the conclusion to "Action de carême/Pain pour le prochain," in *Réhabiliter l'argent* (Lausanne, 1984). This brochure is anonymous, but André Biéler undoubtedly had a great hand in it.

7. Commentary on Ps. 104:15 and Hos. 2:8.

8. Commentary on Isa. 30:23.

> Sustainable development . . . contains within it two key concepts, [the second of which is] the idea of limitations imposed by the state of technology and social organization on the environment's ability to meet present and future needs.

If the environment is unable to provide for the needs of the whole human community, it is not because God's generosity has fallen short but because we have failed to organize ourselves properly to ensure that parts of society are not excluded from the feast. Indeed, the commentary on Isaiah 30:23 quoted above continues, "By our vices we shut the bosom of the earth, which would otherwise be laid open to us, and would abundantly yield fruits of every description, that we might be happy."[9] The part of the definition of sustainable development just quoted explicitly mentions future needs. In this respect it also echoes Calvin. Referring to Genesis 1:26 ("Then God said, 'Let us make humankind in our image, according to our likeness; and let them have dominion. . .'"), he says, "The use of the plural number intimates that this authority was not given to Adam only, but to all his posterity as well as to him."[10] Hence, this generation is not entitled to compromise the capacity of the generations that follow to meet their own needs. The passage in the epigraph strongly implies this in several places. The same point is made insofar as "neighbors" refers to the defenseless; future generations are by definition not able to defend themselves against our actions.

We Recognize God's Generosity by Asking Him for What We Need

> The Prophet [Zechariah] expostulates with them that by their unfaithfulness they thrust from themselves the favor which could have been all ready and fitted out for them. We now therefore understand the Prophet's meaning. He bids them to ask the Lord for rain. They ought indeed to have done this of themselves without being reminded; for though Jesus Christ had not yet taught his Church the form of prayer he later did, it should have been as it were naturally rooted in them to ask God for their daily bread; and it is not without reason that he claims to himself the name of Father. The Prophet then does here reprove the Jews for their brutal stupidity—that they did not at the very least ask the Lord for rain.[11]

> We cannot enjoy anything with a good conscience, except we receive it as from the hand of God. And therefore Paul teaches us that in eating and drinking we only sin, unless faith be present [Rom. 14:23].[12]

9. Ibid.
10. Commentary on Gen. 1:26.
11. Commentary on Zech. 10:1.
12. Commentary on Gen. 1:28.

GOD IS THE LORD AND MASTER

Although God offers us all we need and more, for Calvin it is normal that we should pray to him for it. Calvin sees God as the Lord, but more precisely as a feudal lord of whom we are the obliged. After all, feudalism was the usual form of social organization in the world around him. Calvin devoted considerable thought to the foundations of politics, although he was much more concerned with the exercise of authority than with the question how political authorities came to occupy their positions.[13]

A feudal lord was the absolute master of his domain. His vassals and underlings depended upon him utterly; it was their duty to do his bidding. Whatever they produced or achieved was entirely the result of the arrangements he had made and what he had provided to make it possible. The feudal lord liked his position to be acknowledged, and one way of doing that was to ask him explicitly for what one needed. Conversely, for the petitioners to ask was a way for them to assert that they knew their place in the social order, and that could be reassuring for them as well as for their superiors.[14]

According to the principle of noblesse oblige, the good lord distributed what belonged to him generously among his dependents. One feature that distinguishes God from earthly lords, however, is that he does not return to his people what they have produced; rather, he gratuitously gives everything, even in the absence of a human contribution to its production.

God and His Creation

Calvin did not see God as the Great Clockmaker who, having made his machine, could leave it to run on its own according to the immutable laws of its own inner workings. Descartes was to come later (1596–1650), and the phrase "the Great Clockmaker" gained currency mainly during the industrial revolution of the nineteenth century. Nonetheless, Calvin stressed how marvelously the creation is designed:

> When a person, from beholding and contemplating the heavens, has been brought to know God, he will learn also to reflect upon and to admire his wisdom and power as displayed on the face of the earth, not only in general, but even in the least blades of grass.[15]

13. See Marc-Édouard Chenevière, *La pensée politique de Calvin* (Paris: Labor, 1937).
14. This form of social order still exists in many parts of the world; see Edward Dommen, "Paradigms of Governance and Exclusion," *Journal of Modern African Studies* 35, no. 3 (1997): 485–94.
15. Commentary on Ps. 19:1.

God is ever the active governor of his creation:

> We gather . . . how we ought to consider the creation of the world; to wit, that we may know that all things are subject to God, and ruled by his will.[16]

He is, however, not to be confused with his creation:

> I don't mind if people say that nature is God, if they speak with respect and their heart is pure. But the expression is quite improper, since nature is only an order established by God. It is bad and pernicious in such an important matter, where the greatest prudence is required, to thus confuse the majesty of God with the inferior operations of his hands.[17]

If Descartes came after Calvin, Darwin came even later (1809–1882). Calvin was unaware of the argument that creatures adapt to their environment. His view, on the contrary, was that the environment responds to the needs of creatures:

> The order of nature is thus organized so that all the animals have recourse to their Creator. . . . In this passage [Ps. 145:15] God draws our attention to his admirable arrangements, that there is a certain season appointed for haymaking, harvest and vintage, and that the year is so divided into intervals, that the animals are fed at one time upon grass, at another on hay, or straw, and also acorns, or other products of the earth. Were the whole supply poured forth at one and the same moment, it would be very awkward to deal with them; and we have no small reason to admire the seasonableness with which the different kinds of food for people and beasts are yearly produced.[18]

In another passage he goes into a detailed disquisition on how the seasonal pattern of rain varies from one place to another, and yet always corresponds to the needs of the plants that grow in those very places.[19] He points out that according to Jeremiah and Joel, this does not happen by accident: God gives the rain in the right season. The result may sound quaint to our ears, but it is understandable in the context of the state of the natural sciences in the sixteenth century. Above all, Calvin sticks very close to his ultimate authority, the Bible.

Joel 2:23 is a pregnant passage in this regard. The King James Version renders it, "Rejoice in the LORD your God: for he hath given you the former rain moderately." The *Traduction oecuménique de la Bible* has an extensive note on this passage: "This is sometimes translated as 'rain in just measure,' or 'rain

16. Commentary on Acts of the Apostles, 4:24.
17. *Institutes,* 1.5.5
18. Commentary on Ps. 145:15.
19. Commentary on Joel 2:23.

according to justice,' i.e., according to God's justice, in conformity with the covenant; but it seems preferable to see in this word a term of salvation."[20]

God Has Entrusted the Creation to Humanity (Well, Almost)

> Man has been created by God on the condition that he should be lord over the earth, gathering its fruits, and learning from day to day by experience that the world is subject to him. [He is like] God's vice-regent in the government of the world.[21]

> [However,] man had already been created with this condition, that he should have the earth subject to himself; but . . . he is put in possession of his right, only if he understands what has been given to him by the Lord.[22]

Humanity is a sort of apprentice vice-regent: God does not delegate to humans the full freedom to run the earth on their own. God is constantly interfering—albeit for educational purposes—to foster humanity's understanding of what it has been given. God decides each and every natural event, with this objective in mind:

> God makes use of the winds as his messengers, turns them hither and thither, calms and raises them whenever he pleases, that by their ministry he may declare his power. . . . And certainly we profit little in the contemplation of the whole of nature, if we do not behold with the eyes of faith that spiritual glory of which an image is presented to us in this world.[23]

> It often happens that even when people have devoted themselves faithfully to the service of God they are pressed down by adversities; yea, that God very often designedly tries their faith by withholding from them for a time his blessing.
>
> It often happens that those who sincerely and from the heart serve God, are deprived of earthly blessings, because God intends to elevate their minds to the hope of eternal and lasting reward. God then designedly withdraws his blessing often from the faithful, that they may hunger and thirst in this world; as though they were wasting all their labor in serving him.

20. *Traduction oecuménique de la Bible* (Paris: Le Cerf–Les Bergers et les Mages, 1975), 1125.

21. Commentary on Gen. 1:8 and 1:26.

22. Commentary on Gen. 1:28.

23. Commentary on Ps.104:4. Other readings of Ps. 104:4 are possible; see the corresponding note in the *Traduction oecuménique de la Bible*. The KJV—where the verse is numbered 104:3—uses the version provided in that note.

> And what the Prophet . . . testifies here respecting the fruitful produce of wine, and corn, and oil, and of other goods of the earth, it was still, as I have said, a stronger confirmation. Now, if any one objects again and says that this was of no value, because a servile and mercenary service does not please God; to this I answer that God does often by such means stimulate men, when he sees them to be extremely tardy and slothful, and that he afterwards leads them by other means to serve him truly and from the heart.[24]

Calvin is even more explicit in this passage:

> God does not consider, in chastising the faithful, what they deserve; but what will be useful to them in future; and thus fulfills the office of a physician rather than of a judge. Therefore, the absolution which he imparts to his children is complete and not by halves. That he, nevertheless, punishes those who are received into favor, is to be regarded as a kind of chastisement which serves as medicine for future time, but ought not properly to be regarded as the vindictive punishment of sin committed. . . . If he admonishes in words, he is not heard; if he adds stripes, it avails but little; when it happens that he is heard, the flesh in its pride nevertheless spurns the admonition. . . . Wherefore, this general axiom is to be maintained, that all the sufferings to which human life is subject, are necessary exercises, by which God partly invites us to repentance, partly instructs us in humility, and partly renders us more cautious and more attentive in guarding against the allurements of sin for the future.[25]

Prosperity Is Not a Reward

It cannot be sufficiently stressed that Calvin's argument has nothing whatever to do with the theology of prosperity. The passages quoted at length above in no way argue that good fortune rewards the good and adversity punishes the wicked. God can inflict adversity on the good in order to help them understand that whatever they have is a gratuitous gift from him.

Furthermore, Calvin makes it clear again and again, for instance by using the second person plural rather than the singular, that God's rebukes may be provoked by collective as well as by individual misbehavior, and aimed at the edification of communities rather than of individuals. Thus, commenting on Joel 2:25, which addresses the people as a whole in the second person plural, Calvin in turn insistently uses the same person: "So then, once God will be appeased toward you, and he will be well-disposed toward you, the land itself will do its duty, and nothing more will hinder you from enjoying its abundance."[26]

24. Commentary on Hag. 2:19.
25. Commentary on Gen. 3:19.
26. Commentary on Joel 2:25.

NATURE MAY BE RESTORED

Since the limitations on the environment's ability to meet the needs of humanity are part of an educational process arising from human sinfulness, the restoration of nature to its fullness can be foreseen when humanity is fully reconciled with God:

> He means that everything shall be fully restored, when Jesus Christ shall reign. For we know that all the afflictions of the present life flow from the sin of the first man. We are deprived of the dominion and sovereignty which God had given to man over animals of every kind. At first all of them bowed willingly to the dominion of man; but now the most of them rise up against man, and war against each other. Thus, when wolves, lions, bears and other animals of that kind are hurtful to man and to other beasts from which we obtain benefit and use, and when even animals which ought to have been useful to man cause him trouble, this must be imputed to his sin, because his disobedience has overthrown the order of things. But since it is the office of Jesus Christ to bring back everything to its condition and order, that is the reason why he declares that the confusion or ruin that now exists in human affairs shall be removed by the coming of Jesus Christ. The lion will live without doing harm and will no longer chase after prey. The serpent, satisfied with his dust, shall wrap himself in it, and shall no longer hurt by his envenomed bite. In a word, all that is disordered or confused shall be restored to its proper order.[27]

It would be nice to draw from this the conclusion that as humanity strives to achieve the kingdom of God on earth, so by the same token it will restore the condition of nature to the original beauty, peace, and abundance with which the Creator endowed it. That would, unfortunately, not correspond to Calvin's view of human nature as being not only unregenerate but incapable of regeneration by its own efforts. In the subtitle to the section of his book from which this passage is drawn, Biéler accurately captures Calvin's understanding: "Nature moves forwards towards its liberation at the end of the ages." It is not in historical time but at the end of the ages that nature will be restored.

WHAT SHOULD WE DO AT PRESENT?

Do No Damage

With respect to the creation, Calvin entirely subscribes to the Hippocratic principle, *primum non nocere*: "If there is one thing we must do, it is to do no

27. Commentary on Isa. 65:25.

damage" (see epigraph). The injunction is included in the particularly intriguing phrase in the epigraph concerning "damag[ing] trees and houses and similar things." A present-day ecologist may be surprised to find trees and houses mentioned in the same breath, conceiving of the one as natural and the other as man-made. Calvin was not so prompt to leap to such a classification. Trees are often planted or at least tended by people. Fruit trees—and it is probably these in particular that he has in mind—are planted like a crop where they are needed to supply food. The same goes to a significant extent for firewood and building timber. Conversely, a house may be a feature of the landscape that has been around since before the present occupants arrived. In both cases, these are, above all, elements of God's generous gift of creation and are not radically different from each other.

Be Moderate in Our Requirements

Current-day ecological thinking often refers to the "ecological footprint," to the burden people impose on the environment.[28] To tread lightly, to make moderate demands on the environment, is an important way of expressing one's care for it. Calvin insists on moderation, denouncing waste:

> For nature is content with a little and all that goes beyond natural usage is superfluous. Not that using things a bit freely should be condemned as bad in itself, but greed is always perverse.[29]

> Here are [James's] strictures on the insatiable plundering by the rich, hiding away anything they can pull in, to let it rot uselessly in their coffers. With the result that like enemies of humankind they spoil what God created for human use.[30]

In the *Institutes* Calvin explains the position at much greater length:

> Christian freedom tells us that we are not bound before God to any observance of external things which are in themselves indifferent, but that we are now at full liberty either to use or do without them. The knowledge of this liberty is very necessary to us; where it is wanting our consciences will have no rest, there will be no end of superstition. For when once the conscience is entangled in the net, it enters a long and inextricable labyrinth and a deep pit, from which it is afterwards most difficult to escape. When a man begins to doubt whether it is lawful for him to use linen for sheets, shirts, napkins, and handker-

28. William E. Rees and Mathis Wackernagel, *Our Ecological Footprint: Reducing Human Impact on the Earth* (Philadelphia: New Society Publishers, 1996).
29. Commentary on 1 Tim. 6:7.
30. Commentary on Jas. 5:2.

> chiefs, he will not long be sure as to hemp, and will at last have doubts as to tow; for he will revolve in his mind whether he cannot sup without napkins, or dispense with handkerchiefs. Should he deem a daintier food unlawful, he will afterwards feel uneasy for using brown bread and common eatables, because he will think that his body might possibly be supported on a still meaner food. If he hesitates as to a more genial wine, he will scarcely drink the worst or spoiled wine with a good conscience; at last he will not dare to touch water if more than usually sweet and pure. In fine, he will come to this, that he will deem it criminal to trample on a straw lying in his way.[31]

> We see in short whither this liberty tends, viz. that we are to use the gifts of God without any scruple of conscience, without any perturbation of mind, for the purpose for which he gave them: in this way our souls may both have peace with him, and recognize his liberality towards us.[32]

We shall return to the purpose for which God gives his gifts. Here let us stress that Calvin is most evidently arguing against worrying about what one consumes. He is warning on the one hand against ostentatious nonconsumption (what some might call the Birkenstock lifestyle), which is a paradoxical form of conformist consumerism, but he is also warning against the more conventional consumerism of keeping up with the Joneses. We should take God's gifts as they come, so that we are free to concentrate on doing the work God intends for us rather than frittering away our time on consumption (or nonconsumption) decisions.[33] An incidental effect of that way of managing one's affairs is that we are more attentive to the social as well as economic consequences of our lifestyle. Furthermore, we are likely to tread more lightly on the creation, if only because we allow ourselves less time to put our feet down hard.

Let the Creation Rest: The Sabbath

The Sabbath expresses the requirement to tread lightly because God has better things for us to do: "The believers are to rest from their own works so as to allow God to work in them."[34] In the context of attitudes to the environment, the Sabbath has the further virtue of affording rest to the creation. Just as God has liberated us from slavery—from the status of mere factors of production—so his generosity makes it unnecessary for us to push creation to the limits of its productive capacity: "As people and cattle rested on every seventh day, so

31. *Institutes* (1560), 3.19.7.
32. *Institutes* (1560), 3.19.8.
33. See Edward Dommen, *Quaker Simplicity* (Sunderland: University of Sunderland, Centre for Quaker Studies, 1997).
34. *Institutes* (1560), 2.8.28.

God prescribed that the earth should rest on the seventh year."[35] Indeed, Calvin echoes the threatening tone of the Old Testament to stress this message:

> To this precept he alludes, when he threatens by the Prophets that the land shall enjoy its rest when it has vomited its inhabitants, for since they had polluted it by violating the Sabbath (2 Chronicles 36:21) until it groaned as if under heavy burden, he says that it shall rest for a long continuous period, so as to compensate for the labor it endured for so many years.[36]

WE GLORIFY GOD BY LOOKING AFTER OUR NEIGHBOR

I stated at the start of this essay that Calvin's argument proceeds in two stages. The first is that God created all things for the benefit of humanity. The second stage is that God created humanity to glorify him. The only way we can do that is to reach him where we can—that is, as Matthew 25:31–46 illustrates, in the poor and the weak. With respect to that passage, Calvin reminds us that "God accepts everything given to the poor as being given to himself."[37]

Calvin's argument is echoed at the pivotal passage in the World Commission on Environment and Development's definition of sustainable development: "Sustainable development . . . contains within it two key concepts, [the first being] the concept of 'needs,' in particular the essential needs of the world's poor, to which overriding priority should be given" (see the appendix). We are here at the heart of sustainable development.

In this perspective, Calvin presents his argument in particular in his commentary on 2 Corinthians 8:15, which in turn refers to the manna that is the subject of Exodus 16:

> We do not now have an omer or other fixed measure prescribed by God for the food we have each day, but he has commended to us frugality and temperance and has forbidden us from debauching ourselves when we are in abundance. Thus those who have riches, whether inherited or won by their own industry and labor, let them remember that what is left over is meant not for intemperance or luxury but for relieving the needs of the brethren.[38]

35. Commentary on Exod. 23:10.

36. Commentary on Exod. 23:10. The author of the passage from 2 Chronicles is quoting Lev. 26:32–35, completed by Jer. 25:11 or 29:10 (see note to 2 Chr. 36:21 in the *Traduction oecuménique de la Bible*).

37. Commentary on 1 Tim. 6:18.

38. Commentary on 2 Cor. 8:15.

> We should have no doubt that riches which are heaped up at the expense of our brethren are accursed and will soon perish and their owner will be ruined with them, so that we are not to imagine that the way to grow rich is to make provision for our own distant future and defraud our poor brethren of the help that is their due.[39]

In the latter paragraph lies a hint of the first sentence of the definition of sustainable development. Not only is claiming for ourselves too much of God's creation a violation of the requirement to give overriding priority to the needs of the world's poor, but it is a futile waste.

CONCLUSION

In short, Calvin had relatively little to say about the environment in the narrow sense in which some present-day environmentalists take it. Calvin is in particular at odds with those environmentalists who claim that it is more important to preserve the environment for future generations than to meet the needs of today's poor.

On the other hand, the twentieth-century concept of sustainable development has captured many essential aspects of Calvin's thought. We do not live in a world threatened by shortages; we live in one where maldistribution rooted in the selfishness of the rich deprives the poor of what rightfully belongs to them, a world where the environment's ability to meet present and future needs can be released by means of appropriate technology and social organization. Our overriding obligation is to allow the world's poor to meet their needs, which are urgent and must be met now, not later: "They are like murderers if they see their neighbors wasting away and yet do not open their hands to help them. In this, I tell you, they are certainly like murderers."[40]

All this calls for a detached attitude by the rich toward their own consumption, and this firstly puts less pressure on the environment and secondly leaves space for others, including future generations, to determine and meet their own needs.

39. Ibid.
40. Sermon 44 on Matthew 3:9–10.

APPENDIX

Sustainable Development

Sustainable development is development that meets the needs of the present without compromising the ability of future generations to meet their own needs. It contains within it two key concepts:

> 1. the concept of "needs," in particular the essential needs of the world's poor, to which overriding priority should be given; and
>
> 2. the idea of limitations imposed by the state of technology and social organization on the environment's ability to meet present and future needs
>
> World Commission on Environment and Development, *Our Common Future* (Oxford: Oxford University Press, 1987), 43

5

A General Overview of the Reception of Calvin's Social and Economic Thought

Eberhard Busch

John Calvin's understanding of society and economics is not easily grasped. In the first place, it can only be understood in light of Calvin's concept of the church; in the second place, our perception of his position on both of these fronts, along with much else in his teaching, has been muddied by the work of notable scholars in past generations. Typically the blame here alights upon Max Weber, but I would like to single out some others as particularly at fault. Let us take up these topics—Calvin's two concepts and past (mis)representations of them—in reverse order.

CLASSIC INTERPRETATIONS BESIDES MAX WEBER'S

Albrecht Ritschl's interpretation of Calvin is simply a misinterpretation.[1] Ritschl says that, over against the Lutheran doctrine that contrasts the church as an organ of grace with the government as an organ of order backed by the power of punishment, Calvin blurred the distinction between the two. In this way, he says, Calvin fell into deep errors, although these are errors that one can hardly effect at the same time—on the one hand, monkish flight from the world; on the other, the rule of the church over the government. Calvin's position,

1. See A. Ritschl, "Luthertum und Calvinismus," in *Geschichte des Pietismus*, vol. 1 (Bonn, 1880), 61–80.

continues Ritschl, is identical with the possibility of the removal of a despot by the people, and as such reflects the idea of the French Revolution that everyone is equal before the law (in contrast to a healthier German concept of rule by the proper authorities). This rendition of Calvin's teaching is so clearly a set of prejudices that it is astonishing that it was ever taken seriously. But it is reflected even in the *Ethics* of Dietrich Bonhoeffer: In contrast to the western countries, with their Calvinistic ideas about democracy, sin is taken seriously among the Christians in Germany. This means: "If no one dares to be superior, if no one 'thinks he needs' to be inferior, or if superiority seeks its foundation only in the inferior . . . and if inferiority therefore . . . is understood to be the explosive of all superiority, there already is the beginning of ethical chaos. . . . The genuine order of superior and inferior draws its life from belief in the commission from 'above.'"[2]

Jacob Burckhardt takes quite another critical tack against Calvin, also in reference to his social ideas. Burckhardt thinks that Calvin introduced an undemocratic "ethical chaos" to Geneva. His rule there amounted to "the tyranny of a single human who makes his private notions a general law and gags or chases away all other opinions and offends everybody every day in the most innocent matters of taste"—which tyranny, Burckhardt judged, "has never been outdone in history."[3] Burckhardt's biographer, Basel historian Werner Kaegi, wanted to soften this criticism but in fact intensified it when he cast Calvin as Dostoyevsky's "Grand Inquisitor."[4] Burckhardt wanted to shock his pious contemporaries in Basel with his thesis, and to that end he used source material that members of the traditional families of Geneva had gathered against Calvin expressing sympathy with the patriarchal government of Bern, a move these traditionalists made mainly because they saw in Calvin an importunate foreigner who was befriending a crowd of additional foreigners who would change Genevan customs.

Shocking the good people of Basel was not foreign either to the work of Karl Barth, who was related to Burckhardt. In his 1922 lecture on "Calvin's Theology," Barth describes Calvin as a figure of a "shocking tragedy," an "all-consuming fire," to whom God's will was "the will to power" and by which he in fact came to power in Geneva in 1555.[5] We cannot describe the system of life Calvin decreed for the people in his town, Barth declared, "without such

2. D. Bonhoeffer, *Ethics*, ed. E. Bethge (New York: Macmillan, 1955), 242, 257.

3.Quoted in W. Kaegi, *Jacob Burckhardt: Eine Biographie*, vol. 5 (Basel: B. Schwabe & Co., 1947), 90. The translation is my own.

4. Ibid., 98.

5. K. Barth, *Die Theologie Calvins: Vorlesung Gottingen Sommersemester 1922*, ed. H. Scholl (Zurich: Theologischer Verlag, 1993), 164, 153, 157.

words as tyranny and pharisaism coming instinctively to our lips. None of us . . . would have liked to live in that town."[6] Barth later learned to see Calvin in another light, but his distance remained.

Ernst Troeltsch has yet another opinion of Calvin. First of all, he wants to distinguish between Calvin and Calvinism more than did Max Weber.[7] For him, Calvin is close to Luther, from whom Calvin departed by making predestination the crucial dogma.[8] But Troeltsch's interpretation is not without ambiguities: that the ideal of the early church meant its reign over the state,[9] or that Calvin paid homage to individualism but wished to establish a holy congregation,[10] or that in his theology the Decalogue disappeared into natural law,[11] or that predestination became concrete for him in the idea of the vocation of the best to rule over the others.[12] All this scarcely shows familiarity with Calvin's texts, quite apart from the inconsistency of these various statements. Still, Troeltsch's observations of the social consequences of Calvin's theology are interesting. Though he believes that austerity worked effectively for the increase of capital, he disputes "that capitalism derives from Calvinism."[13] Though, according to Troeltsch, Calvin's idea of the "same rule of law over everybody" encouraged "the cultivation of independent personality" in its "initiative and sense of responsibility for action," this "combined also with a very strong sense of unity for common, positive ends and values, which are invulnerable on account of their religious character."[14] According to Troeltsch, here is the root of Calvin's interest in the international ties of a "union of Christian nations."[15] Here also is the source of a tendency in his thoughts toward a "Christian socialism," what German Lutheranism called an "interference in purely secular matters."[16] The notion of a *Christian* socialism is of course unclear; it does not have the anti-Semitic meaning Adolf Stoecker gave it under this title.

Finally I mention Charles Hodge, who was influential in the United States in the nineteenth century. His "Calvinism" in fact proceeded according to the Lutheran two-kingdom doctrine. Perhaps this conservative understanding of Calvin explains the indifference to Calvin on the part of the American Christian

6. Ibid., 163.
7. E. Troeltsch, *Die Soziallehren der christlichen Kirchen und Gruppen*, in *Gesammelte Schriften*, vol. 1 (Tübingen: Mohr, 1912), 656.
8. Ibid., 615.
9. Ibid., 620–21.
10. Ibid., 623–25.
11. Ibid., 658.
12. Ibid., 669.
13. Ibid., 716, 713.
14. Ibid., 671.
15. Ibid., 670.
16. Ibid., 721.

socialist Walter Rauschenbusch.[17] Hodge emphasizes that the church "has nothing to do with the state. . . . She has nothing to do with tariffs, or banks, or internal improvements. We say . . . : 'Let the dead bury the dead.'. . . She has nothing to do as a Church with secular affairs." Yet suddenly a new tone emerges: "To adopt any theory which would stop the mouth of the Church, and prevent her bearing her testimony to kings and rulers, magistrates and people, in behalf of the truth and law of God, is like administrating chloroform to a man to prevent his doing mischief."[18] In his *Lectures on Calvinism* delivered in Princeton in 1898, Abraham Kuyper reflected Hodge's ideas: on the one hand he distinguished strongly between the church and the state, culture, and economics; on the other he saw both of them directly subject to God's sovereignty.[19] In this way he wanted to distance himself from many other concepts, such as have been repeated in our own times: from socialism and capitalism, from the French Revolution, and from dialectical theology.[20] One can, in sum, share W. Stanford Reid's opinion on earlier works about Calvin: that they judge Calvinism "very often without bothering to go back to see what he actually said."[21]

THE ORGANIZATION OF THE CHURCH ACCORDING TO CALVIN

I do at least adopt one dictum of L. F. Schulze in South Africa: "Calvin did not speak as an economist but as a theologian."[22] But a theologian in which sense? I think in the sense that he discussed social and economic affairs, among other matters, but he always spoke about them as a theologian. This does not mean that he founded a bibliocracy, as Gregg Singer maintains.[23] Rather, it means that Calvin's attention was mainly directed to the problem of the organization

17. Calvin is not mentioned in Rauschenbusch's *Christianity and the Social Crisis* (New York: Hodder and Stoughton, 1911) and is mentioned only briefly in his *Selected Writings*, ed. W. S. Hudson (New York and Mahwah, NJ: Paulist Press, 1984), 173.

18. C. Hodge, *Discussions in Church Polity* (New York: Charles Scribner's, 1878), 104–6.

19. A. Kuyper, *Calvinism: Six Stone-lectures* (1898; repr., Grand Rapids: Eerdmans, 1931).

20. L. F. Schulze, "Calvin on Interest and Property: Some Aspects of His Socio-Economic View," in *Calvin's Thought on Economic and Social Issues and the Relationship of Church and State*, ed. R. C. Gamble (New York: Garland Pub., 1992), 185–96.

21. W. S. Reid, "Early Critic of Capitalism (II)," in R. C. Gamble, *Calvin's Thought*, 169.

22. Schulze, "Calvin on Interest and Property," 225.

23. C. G. Singer, "Calvin and the Social Order, or Calvin as a Social and Economic Statesman," in R. C. Gamble, *Calvin's Thought*, 236.

of the church and that in his clarification of the different responsibilities of church and state he stressed certain social and economic accents. Unlike Luther and Zwingli he, as a Reformer of the second generation, understood the question of the *ecclesiae disciplina* as decisive. In view of the danger facing the Huguenots, Calvin taught that the church must stand on its own two feet in relation to its own *order* as well as in other matters, even where there exists a spirit of harmony between church and society. For in each social system the church is the right church only when its message, like its order, is founded on the word of God. The church order is not regarded as *jus divinum*. It is *jus humanum*, but in this way—that it is responsible to the *jus divinum*. Therefore, the church order has to manifest certain structures that bear witness to its foundation in the divine order. But at the same time it leaves room so that within those structures the shaping of the church order may adapt to that which is possible and that makes sense in each particular case. This allows a flexibility, so that the church order in Scotland or in Hungary may be other than in Geneva, while at the same time the different churches remain Reformed.

What is the basic structure of the church order? It is not given by an idea or a historical tradition. It is a spiritual reality given by God in Jesus Christ. The indicative precedes the imperative here. This reality is given by Christ as the head of his body, which is the congregation. Both belong together but in such a way that Christ is not ruled by the congregation; rather, his congregation is ruled by him. It is founded by him and is nourished by him. But if Christ is the head of his body, what about the human government of the church? Calvin was much engaged with this question, but not because his doctrine of the church is mainly concerned with its government; rather, because he sees this as the decisive point for dealing with the Roman Catholic doctrine of the church. Calvin appears to present only a formal change when he rests the human correspondence to the three functions of Christ as priest, king, and prophet in the church not on the shoulders of *one* person alone but on the shoulders of *several*.[24] In fact, this changes the whole understanding of the church. By this it becomes clear that Christ *alone* is the head of his congregation. The offices in it stand below the head; they are not above the congregation, but within it. They work in the service of the head of the congregation, and they do so in a human correspondence with Christ.

In the human exercise of the three offices, the offices get a new content. Since Christ alone is the head of the congregation, human action only testifies to his threefold office; it does not complete it. The ministers are not priests; they perform together with the teachers the prophetic office of interpreting Scripture. To the priesthood of Christ corresponds the service of the

24. *Institutes* 2.15; 4.4.1.

deacons and their support for the poor. And to Christ's office as king corresponds the office of the elders, with their task of pastoral care for church members in accordance with Christian community. In this the Reformed practice of home visitation is historically rooted. And because the church offices correspond only to a *human* degree to the government by Christ in the Holy Spirit, therefore rules pertaining to them do not correspond to the one-sided relation of the head to his body. Some controlling functions are therefore necessary if the human duty of leading the church is to be done appropriately. This is achieved, for instance, by mutual inquiries (*censura morum*) among church leaders about their conduct. In principle such an understanding of the congregation allows all church members to share in its controlling functions, because according to Calvin all Christians participate in Christ's threefold office through their faith.[25]

What is the reality of Christ's body as he wishes that body to be? It is that the church be a congregation of brothers and sisters. Calvin explains this in a way that brings the notions of community and individual existence in relation with each other. The individual Christian is a member of Christ's body. Thus, he or she takes part in Christ the head and in execution of Christ's threefold office, and does so both passively and actively. Via active participation in Christ, every Christian is a mature Christian and so a responsible member of the congregation. Christian individuals are therefore not Christians for themselves but in the Christian community. It becomes clear as a result that each church member takes part in the threefold office of Christ with a particular task, just as the members of the body have particular tasks and in this way are in harmony. This participation points to the lively richness of the congregation but also to the need to supplement the witness of the individual Christian. According to Calvin, the Christian congregation is the community of brothers and sisters in the mutuality of their communication with one another.

SOCIAL AND ECONOMIC ORGANIZATION ACCORDING TO CALVIN

It might now be clear that Calvin understands the organization of the social and economic sphere as analogous to the church, in which Christians live in community and in individual responsibility beneath Christ as the one head. He sees the social and economic sphere as an institution for the support of a life in public weal and freedom—that is, public weal but not at the expense of freedom, and freedom but not at the expense of public weal. Recent studies on Calvin have

25. Catechism of Geneva (1545), Questions 34–45.

emphasized this point, although they have not explicitly stressed the importance of the church for Calvin in grounding this concept. Nor have they only reread the well-known Calvin texts that are fundamental for our question; they have also discovered previously unnoticed passages, especially from his numerous sermons. In these, Calvin as a theological interpreter of the Bible expresses a particular social and economic responsibility. He is not misusing the Bible for his private taste but drawing on it as a word for the contemporary situation. His sermons are the source of his commentaries and open the gate to research upon them.

This approach shows how Calvin holds a prophetic office in a precise sense of the term. On the one hand, it has led recent scholarship to look as closely as possible into the socioeconomic situation and changes in Geneva per se in the middle of the sixteenth century; on the other hand, it has helped us to understand that Calvin's remarks have a critical tone, as Stephen Reid stresses: "He is a critic of an existing system, rather than an advocate or founder of a new one." "In practical terms," Reid continues, this means that "Calvinism in Geneva was more an attack upon poverty than an advocacy of capital accumulation."[26]

Robert Kingdon raised the question about what was new in Geneva in Calvin's time as compared with the Middle Ages.[27] Relief services for the poor already existed; what changed in Geneva was that the services were rationalized and carried out by laymen. Mark Valeri explains that, according to Calvin, economy and the ethics of the public weal must work together. Accordingly, when Calvin opposes the competitive form of human relations, he stands against the trend of the economy in his time and maybe in every time.[28] He especially fights against usury, and when usury hides under ever new labels, the fight becomes one against the misuse of the language in favor of reliability.[29] This prophet does not fight as a man of rigid views, however, but as a theologian whose ethics knows the difference between lending and usury and bears a spirit of compromise. In all this, Calvin is engaged for the purpose of social solidarity. Valeri summarizes Calvin's diagnosis of the problem: "Dissolution of the bonds of communication . . . [isolates] individuals from others in the body social, resulting in the misuse of neighbor as an object for gain."[30] In the same vein, Jane Dempsey Douglass writes that, according to Calvin, "restored humanity is not individual but social." All are created equal *and* for one

26. S. Reid, "John Calvin, Early Critic of Capitalism (1)," in R. C. Gamble, *Calvin's Thought*, 161–63.

27. R. Kingdon, "Calvinism and Social Welfare," *Calvin Theological Journal* 17 (1982): 212–30.

28. M. Valeri, "Religion, Discipline, and the Economy in Calvin's Geneva," *Sixteenth Century Journal* 28, no. 1 (1997): 139.

29. Ibid., 137.

30. Ibid., 138.

another; where people live against this principle, they bear a mark of sin and invite God's wrath.[31] Certainly, Calvin is interested in individual responsibility, but apparently he also sees a correspondence to the mutuality in Christ's body in the mutuality required of the members of the council and the elders of the church in their public responsibility in Geneva.

As these studies have shown, there were two concerns above all on which Calvin concentrated in performing his prophetic task in Geneva. To put it more clearly, there were two miseries that, in his view, disturbed living together and put social solidarity to a severe test. The first involved the relation of residents to foreigners, which became a problem among the people of Geneva very rapidly. Previously it was the rule that each town had to look after its own needy residents. But now there arrived in Geneva crowds of French refugees who had been expelled from their own country. In a few years the number of inhabitants in Geneva nearly doubled, and because the space in the city narrowed and the question of livelihood became urgent, it became a highly practical question whether strangers are our neighbors. Perhaps part of the annoyance Geneva's traditional families felt toward Calvin was rooted in his giving an affirmative answer to this question, in his remaining himself a foreigner for a long time in Geneva, and in the government of the city coming into the hands of the foreigners around 1555.[32] The "foreigners" were first refugees from France, but that slowly opened the door for others from Italy and England; Kingdon notes that help was given also to a Turk and a Jew.[33] Valeri quotes a sermon on Deuteronomy in which Calvin speaks about his meeting with a stranger: "Even if we cannot speak a single word to one another, our Lord shows us today that we will be brothers, because Christ is the peace of the whole world and of all peoples. Therefore we must live together in a family of brothers and sisters which Christ has founded in his blood; and with every hostility he gives the opportunity to resist hostility."[34]

The other misery that according to Calvin puts social solidarity to a hard test is the disproportion between the poor and the rich. The culture of the Middle Ages recognized donations for the poor as good work, and since to allow for the opportunity to do good works it was no problem that the poor remained poor, poverty itself could become an ideal for the saints. Over against this, Calvin understood poverty as an unbearable scandal, and this in the sorry form to which Nicholas Wolterstorff refers: Social injustice and the tears of

31. J. D. Douglass, "Calvin's Relation to Social and Economic Change," *Church and Society* 14 (March–April 1984), 127.

32. Valeri, "Religion, Discipline, and the Economy," 128.

33. Kingdon, "Calvinism and Social Welfare," 228.

34. Quoted in Valeri, "Religion, Discipline, and the Economy," 139.

the social victims wound God, too. That human beings bear God's image means that God sees himself in our victimized co-human. But in the vulnerable love of God is rooted also the struggle for justice.[35] Therefore, according to Calvin the task of the rich is not done via donations; rather, as Valeri quotes Calvin, "I cannot separate myself from those who come in need to whom God has knit me." In such a solidarity one can see conversely also the scandal of the luxury of the rich in the metropolises. This luxury is an expression of "self-seeking."[36] The self-denial that is the subject of Calvin's doctrine of sanctification does not mean either a virtue that is valuable in itself or a lack of any sense for joy in life, but the active, helpful countermovement against the "self-seeking" of the rich. It means as well a sharing of the goods of the rich with the poor in the hope that this will build a society of solidarity that lives and can live in a mutual giving and receiving.

As shown by recent research, the rich refugees from France also became involved in that sharing with the poor, with the aim of creating social solidarity so that poverty did not become the fate of some people by consequence of competition. This confirms, finally, what Troeltsch stresses: that Calvin's plea for a "balance of community and individual" in social policy went in the "opposite" direction from the classical capitalist theory of Adam Smith.[37] While in Lutheranism socialism is regarded as "an attack on all holy foundations of the God-given order," says Troeltsch, this tradition of Calvin lives again in the present time in the Reformed domain among the so-called "socialistic Clergymen."[38]

Let us conclude by letting Calvin speak for himself. In his sermon on Galatians 6:9–11, Calvin brings the two sides, the poor and the foreigners, together: "We cannot but behold our own face as it were in a glass in the person that is poor and despised . . . though he were the furthest stranger in the world. Let a Moor or a Barbarian come among us, and yet inasmuch as he is a human, he brings with him a looking glass wherein we may see that he is our brother and neighbor."[39] I think this concrete spiritual insight is the source of Calvin's interest in social and economic affairs. He wrote in his commentary on 2 Corinthians 8:13ff.: "God wills that there be proportion and equality among us, that is, each man is to provide for the needy according to the extent of his means so that no one has too much and no one has too little."[40]

35. N. Wolterstorff, "The Wounds of God: Calvin's Theology of Social Injustice," *Reformed Journal* 16 (June 1987): 14–22.

36. Quoted in Valeri, "Religion, Discipline, and the Economy," 137n39.

37. Troeltsch, "Die Soziallehren der christlichen Kirchen und Gruppen," 676, 717.

38. Ibid., 721.

39. Cited in Woltersdorff, "The Wounds of God," 18.

40. Quoted in A. Biéler, *The Social Humanism of Calvin*, trans. P. T. Fuhrmann (Richmond: John Knox Press, 1964), 33.

PART 2

Calvin's Global Influence

6

Abraham Kuyper's Calvinism

Society, Economics, and Empire in the Late Nineteenth Century

James D. Bratt

Abraham Kuyper (1837–1920) makes an apt test case for the questions raised in this book. On the religious side, Calvinism has never had a stronger, more persistent champion than this late-nineteenth-century Dutch Renaissance man. Kuyper credited Calvinist theology as the instrument of his own salvation and devoted much labor to rehabilitating its doctrine. Moreover, he thought that its inner principles generated the complete worldview that was necessary to meet the challenges of modernity, and within that worldview he formulated a social and political philosophy that he traced back through the Reformed masters to the hand of Calvin himself. Further, Kuyper was not just a speaker of these words but a doer also. He was the founder of the Netherlands' first mass political party (the Antirevolutionary Party), the founder of an intentionally Reformed university (the Vrije Universiteit of Amsterdam), the key organizer of a complete system of Christian elementary and secondary schools, a key supporter of a Protestant labor union, and the founder, and for half a century the editor, of a mass-circulation newspaper (Holland's first) by which he promoted these causes among a national audience of *kleine luyden*, or lower-middle-class and skilled-working-class devotees of classic Reformed orthodoxy.[1]

Kuyper's work came at a crucial epoch in Dutch history. Entering the public stage in 1870 and leaving it only with his death in 1920, Kuyper witnessed

1. For a brief overview in English, see James D. Bratt, *Abraham Kuyper: A Centennial Reader* (Grand Rapids: Eerdmans, 1998), 1–16.

the beginnings and fleshing out of industrialization in the national economy; championed the democratization of its politics, the differentiation of its society, and the pluralization of its public culture; urgently reassessed policies toward the East Indies (the fruit of the Netherlands' seventeenth-century imperialism); and protested the conquest of his belatedly discovered kinfolk in South Africa at the hands of Great Britain amid the renewed imperial competition at the turn of the twentieth century.[2] Kuyper looked back fondly upon the Dutch "golden age," whose glories he attributed to the Calvinist spirit but whose finances were provided by what we can denominate the first wave of modern globalization, featuring commodity exchange in sailing ships. He lived amid the second-wave globalization of industrialism and European territorial conquest in Africa and Asia. From his example perhaps we can draw instruction for our own third-wave globalization of an information economy run by multinational corporations and regulatory agencies.

Kuyper was born in a manse of the Dutch Reformed Church (Nederlandse Hervormde Kerk) and educated at Leiden from gymnasium through a doctorate in theology. His father seems to have been cautious and moderate in opinion as well as temperament; young Abraham was the opposite. At university Kuyper came under the influence of J. H. Scholten, the pioneer of Dutch theological modernism, and while he eventually came to oppose that position, he persisted in Scholten's pattern of bold, rigorous, and systematic thinking. Likewise, he absorbed from Matthias de Vries, the international champion of Dutch literature, the stamp of Romantic poetics. In the middle of his graduate training Kuyper showed his unusual scholarly aptitude by winning a national academic competition on early Reformed ecclesiology sponsored by the theology faculty at the University of Groningen. Groningen had a cultural-nationalist as well as theologically progressive motive for its project, for it bewailed Calvin's influence in the Dutch church and sought to demote him as a foreign import, a French zealot on the tolerant turf of Erasmus. Kuyper's treatise met that end by endorsing instead the ecclesiology of Johannes à Lasco as it had developed among the Dutch exile churches at Emden and London.[3]

But the career ambition that drove Kuyper to win these honors drove him as well to a breakdown from overwork, and then, at the end of his studies, to a tearful conversion from pride and heterodoxy to a generic evangelical-Victorian piety. A few years later, in the mid-1860s, he became convinced of the inadequacy of all such affective, mediating solutions to the challenges of mod-

2. See E. H. Kossmann, *The Low Countries, 1780–1940* (Oxford: Clarendon Press, 1978), 206–438.

3. George Puchinger, *Abraham Kuyper: De jonge Kuyper (1837–1867)* (Franeker: T. Wever, 1987).

ern thought. The defection of some notable Modernist ministers to thoroughgoing philosophical naturalism raised for him the specter of a world gone entirely materialistic in vision, values, and social ethos. He set out to find a Christian alternative and ended at Geneva. In "Calvin himself lay the foundations which, banning all doubt, permitted the edifice of faith to be constructed in a completely logical style." Calvin's system afforded Kuyper's soul "that shelter in the rocks which, being founded on the rock and being hewn from the rock of thought, laughs at every storm."[4]

Tellingly, Kuyper framed this turn in a political, and distinctly populist, context. It was "a small group of malcontents. . .of low social status" in his first, country parish that showed him the virtues of Calvin's thought, he recalled, and it was via their empowerment in church affairs that he anticipated the salvation of the Dutch Reformed Church. The church, too, needed to be converted from halfhearted routine into a moral power of the first order, bringing healing to the nation. Accordingly, Kuyper's first appearance on the national stage came in an 1867 pamphlet that called for the democratization of parish elections. The change was not only fair and equitable, he argued, but would tilt power decisively toward the orthodox, who were plentiful in the rank and file, and away from the Modernists, who survived only in symbiosis with the privileged and powerful. Kuyper's passion aimed, here and hereafter, at least as much against church-administrative elites as against heterodox clergy. In his not unjust indictment, the reorganization of the Dutch church by the Restorationist King Willem I in 1816 had transposed presbyterian order into a hierarchy of classical and synodical boards that operated top-down instead of bottom-up and put institutional efficiency above purity of doctrine and life. In this system, as Kuyper summarized it, irresponsibility above bred apathy in the pew and corruption in podium and pulpit alike. Reformation as well as justice, then, lay in a "return" (a historically inaccurate justification for what was in fact a radical innovation) to a decentralized and lay-driven church polity.[5]

But if reforming the church aimed in no small part at changing national culture, reforming the school followed next and brought Kuyper into civil politics. In the process his tenets of local control and decentralization led to a third

4. Abraham Kuyper, "Confidentially," in Bratt, *Abraham Kuyper*, 57–59. Besides Puchinger, see Johan Stellingwerff, *Dr. Abraham Kuyper en de Vrije Universiteit* (Kampen: Kok, 1987), 21–75; Jasper Vree, *Kuyper in de Kiem* (Hilversum: Verloren, 2006); Jasper Vree, "More Pierson and Mesmer, and less Pietje Baltus: Kuyper's Ideas on Church, State, Society, and Culture during the First Years of His Ministry (1863–1866)," in *Kuyper Reconsidered: Aspects of His Life and Work*, ed. Cornelius van der Kooi and Jan de Bruijn (Amsterdam: VU Uitgeverij, 1999), 299–310.

5. Kuyper, "Confidentially," 55. For the church situation, see A. J. Rasker, *De Nederlandse Hervormde Kerk vanaf 1795* (Kampen: Kok, 1974). Kuyper's first brochure was *Wat Moet Wij Doen?* . . . (Culemborg: A. J. Blom, 1867).

principle, namely, pluralism. The unitary public school system that the Dutch government was trying to maintain inevitably led to problems of conscience or faith, Kuyper argued. To enforce the Reformed monopoly on education, as had been the norm in previous centuries, was unfair to Roman Catholics and Jews, but to water down that model first into generically Protestant, then vaguely theistic, education as different regimes had attempted over the course of the nineteenth century offended strict believers and nonbelievers alike without rendering up an ethical or intellectual framework coherent enough to win the respect of those in between. The only solution was to pluralize education wholesale, to let several systems emerge nationwide—Calvinist, Catholic, humanist or "neutral"—with parents enrolling their children at full public subsidy at the school of their choice.[6]

Educational policy remained the right arm of Kuyper's political movement until he effected the full-subsidy principle during his term as prime minister (1901–1905), a step that pioneered the "pillarization" which distinguished Dutch public life for the first two-thirds of the twentieth century. (That is, different confessional/ideological groups lived in integrated vertical social networks each complete with its own social, cultural, educational, political, communications, and labor organizations.) Early in his career, Kuyper could intimate that this was a pragmatic strategy by which his followers might garner presence and resources enough to work for the reestablishment of Calvinist hegemony in public life, but all along he also declared his to be a principled pluralism, from the rights and for the benefit of every group, and to the ultimate good of the whole. This soon became the settled position of his movement, as he declared before a party convention in 1891:

> Without any craftiness or secret intentions we accept the position of equality before the law along with those who disagree with us and . . . ask for ourselves no other constitutional liberty than that which makes possible the performance of our Christian duty. In the civil state all citizens of the Netherlands must have equal rights before the law. The time must come when it will be considered inconceivable, even ridiculous, to discriminate against or offend anyone, whoever it may be, for his convictions.[7]

If educational policy was Kuyper's right arm in civil politics, then a democratic franchise was the left, and another conjunction of pragmatism and principle. Giving "little people" the vote would swell the returns of the religious parties, Kuyper accurately predicted. Barely ten years after the founding of his

6. F. C. Gerretson, "Dr. Kuyper's Utrechtse Periode (1867–1870)" and "Dr. Kuyper's Utrechtse Tuchtmeester," in *Verzamelde Werken*, vol. 3 (Baarn: Bosch and Keuning, 1973), 238–67.

7. Abraham Kuyper, "Maranatha!" in Bratt, *Abraham Kuyper*, 221.

party, the Calvinist Antirevolutionaries were at the head of the Dutch government in coalition with the Roman Catholic People's Party, and after full adult suffrage was awarded at the end of World War I, that coalition was part of virtually every cabinet for the next seventy-five years. Even more than in church affairs, however, democratization in civil politics was for Kuyper a matter of justice and right, and he pursued it to the point of splitting his own party in the mid-1890s. The course of history was flowing inevitably in this direction, Kuyper told his conservative wing, and those who resisted would drown. A good thing too, he added. Popular democracy, if properly led and channeled, could raise a bulwark against the oppressions of the mighty with which the pages of history abounded and which it was the mission of the Christian church to resist. Kuyper counted it to the Netherlands' shame that it had as late as 1880 one of the most restricted franchises in all of Europe. This undermined national unity, sapped the energy and commitment that were vital for progress, and stifled the forces of reform that always and everywhere flowed upward from the commons to replenish the decadent ranks of leadership.[8]

Why then did Kuyper insist on calling his party "Antirevolutionary" and cite the French Revolution, so commonly deemed the very symbol of democratization, as the font of most evils that Europe was facing in his time? Kuyper first recited the standard conservative answer that "1789" had tried to alter the complex flow of human life all at once and by an abstract plan, but he underscored as well a Christian critique that faulted the Revolution's animating principle of "no God, no master." That is, behind the course of political events lay the secularist Enlightenment revolution in ultimate allegiance and authority away from divine law to human reason. Given human sinfulness, this defiance opened events to the worst possibilities of human nature. Since the Revolution also swept away the protections of custom and tradition in the bargain, society was given over to the strife of each against all, with the spoils going to the strong. The Revolutionary struggle did not achieve liberty then, said Kuyper, but alternating tyrannies of the majority or of a militant faction; not equality, but worse stratification than ever, compounded by the merciless materialism of the triumphant bourgeoisie and their smug self-justifications; not fraternity, but rival nationalisms now armed as never before.[9]

8. On the tensions over pluralism and democratization in Kuyper's movement, see D. T. Kuiper, *De Voormannen* (Meppel: Boom, 1972), 148–230. The history of his party is covered in the essays in George Harinck et al., eds., *De Antirevolutionaire partij, 1829–1980* (Hilversum: Verloren, 2001).

9. Kuyper's most thorough analysis on this point comes in *Niet de Vrijheidsboom maar het Kruis* (Amsterdam: Wormser, 1889). For a capsule summary in English, see Abraham Kuyper, *The Problem of Poverty* (Grand Rapids: Baker, 1991) [ET of *Het Sociale Vraagstuk en de Christelijke Religie* (Amsterdam: J. A. Wormser, 1891), 43–52].

Abuses did not negate true virtues, however, so Kuyper sought to secure liberty by making it congruent with the development of history, the lessons of human nature, and strictures of divine law. He did so by fencing it about with constitutional law and rooting that law in Reformed tradition. As the title of his first major essay in political theory put it, "Calvinism [was the] Source and Stronghold of Our Constitutional Liberties." Kuyper proceeded in this piece backwards from the contemporary United States as the undisputed paragon of liberty (and as the exfoliation of its supposed New England "core") to the English Civil War (expressive of Puritan principle) to the Huguenots in the French wars of religion, with their vesture of the right to resistance in the lesser magistrates, to John Calvin himself. For a professed devotee of historical gradualism, Kuyper's essay rather blithely celebrates revolutionary struggles that, relative to the times, matched the French for ferocity and destruction. For an heir of Dutch Restoration legitimist thought, he rather celebrated Calvin's harshest disparagements of monarchy and concluded that, "given a free choice, Calvin certainly prefers the republic. . . . Entrusting authority to the many decreases the temptations to tyranny." Likewise in church law, Calvin "hovered between aristocracy and democracy," but his legacy pointed clearly in the latter direction.[10]

Kuyper more than once therefore characterized the French Revolution as a secularized parody of Calvinist political reformation. The crucial differences lay along theological and social-ontological lines that crossed at the question of the autonomous individual: The Reformed did and the Revolution did not seek to follow the immutable ordinances God had erected for human life in creation and disclosed in revelation. And the Reformed did, as the Revolution did not, honor the social bonds that were at once the consequence and fabric of those divine ordinations. "The Christian religion seeks personal human dignity in the social relationships of an organically integrated society," Kuyper declared, while "the French Revolution disturbed that organic tissue, broke those social bonds, and left nothing but the monotonous, self-seeking individual asserting his own self-sufficiency."[11] Indeed, social organicism was operationally as strong in Kuyper as his professed starting point of divine law and revelation. It undoubtedly reflected (whether it grew from such in the first place is not certain) the German Romantic thinking he absorbed at university, for throughout his career Kuyper enthusiastically depicted institutions (including churches), movements, nations, and peoples as possessing—even being possessed by—a

10. Abraham Kuyper, "Calvinism: Source and Stronghold of Our Constitutional Liberties" [ET of *Het Calvinisme, oorsprong en waarborg onzer constitutioneele vrijheden* (Amsterdam: B. vander Land, 1874)], in Bratt, *Abraham Kuyper*, quotations 305–6.

11. Kuyper, *Problem of Poverty*, 44.

definitive "germ," "spirit," or "principle" that guided their development toward their inherent destiny. Kuyper sometimes expressed this in a truly progressive, egalitarian form: every people on earth has its own contribution to make, its distinct coloration to add to the glorious rainbow of God's creation, and under God's will none of them could be spared or suppressed. More often he observed the ethnic-racial hierarchies common to contemporary European thought, by which history as a heliotropic force had brought Protestant Europeans to the top of the global pyramid, left Africans at the bottom, driven Amerindians to extinction, and distributed the rest somewhere in between.[12]

His most regular note, however, was a celebration of pluralism or diversity as good in itself, as the mark of a vital, prospering society, and as the creational will of God. Thus, his original political plank about education reflected a cosmic principle at the same time that it harkened back to Kuyper's picture—and a fair bit of the reality—of Dutch social arrangements in the seventeenth-century golden age. That era's complex divisions of political sovereignty among towns, provinces, States General, and Stathouder are one measure of his model; so also its proliferation of craft guilds, merchant corporations, religious societies, militia companies, local dialects, and provincial costumes. Such diversity, such "spontaneous, free-forming life," was not just the mark but the cause of Dutch glory, Kuyper repeated. He attributed his own age's sad departure from that standard to the bourgeois lust for standardization and the Restoration regime's perpetuation, rather than reversal, of the Napoleonic-revolutionary quest for centralized control. His diagnosis and evaluation are captured neatly in the title of his first great cultural address: "Uniformity, the Curse of Modern Life" (1869).[13]

Kuyper cast this picture into a more formal social theory in his most famous oration, "Sphere Sovereignty," delivered at the inauguration of the Free University in 1880. "Our human life," he began, "is neither simple nor uniform but constitutes an infinitely complex organism" that is "so structured that the individual exists only in groups, and only in groups can the whole become manifest." These "parts" he designated "'spheres,' each animated by its own spirit," each ordained by God for the proper ordering and full flourishing of human life, each therefore delegated a portion of God's own absolute, original sovereignty. (Kuyper listed in passing some of these spheres as the personal, domestic, scientific, social, ecclesiastical, intellectual, and religious. In

12. For a typical example of this thinking, see Kuyper, *Lectures on Calvinism* (Grand Rapids: Eerdmans, 1956), 33–40. For a study of the broader issue see J. W. Schulte Nordholt, *The Myth of the West: America as the Last Empire* (Grand Rapids: Eerdmans, 1995).

13. Abraham Kuyper, "Uniformity, the Curse of Modern Life" [ET of *Eenvormigheid, de Vloek van het Moderne Leven* (Amsterdam: H. de Hoogh, 1869)], in Bratt, *Abraham Kuyper*, 19–44.

the next generation the philosophers Herman Dooyeweerd and D. H. Vollenhoven would extend the list to no more or less than fourteen.) No little part of sin, Kuyper continued, lay in the impingement by one sphere on another in defiance of divine will and the human good. The state had been ordained by God to prevent or roll back such sin; as the "sphere of spheres" the state therefore had a noble calling. But it also faced a powerful, chronic temptation. Indeed, "Sphere Sovereignty" opens with a narrative of world history as one continuing quest for unitary empire by the representatives of "State sovereignty"—Asian despots, the Caesars, the Habsburgs—culminating in his own age with the rival pretensions of reactionary (German) and revolutionary (French) state systems. Kuyper's theory thus leaves the resonance of a minor chord. Its secondary notes are the state's divine mandate to protect the individual vis-à-vis her group and to repel any encroachment by one sphere upon another. But its tonic note is his assumption that everywhere and at all times, most especially in his own day, the state tries to absorb all of society into itself. This made the defense of sphere sovereignty, for Kuyper, the defense of divine sovereignty itself.[14]

Kuyper's theory bears strong resemblances to that of Johannes Althusius (1557–1638), so strong that the lack of any citation of the latter by the former is remarkable.[15] Perhaps Kuyper was put off by his own contemporary Otto von Gierke's invocation of Althusius to warrant a federal republican regime for Germany upon a secular Hegelian basis. Or perhaps Althusius's location in Emden brought up the à Lasco connection that Kuyper had forsaken for allegiance to Calvin: better the real Geneva than the "Geneva of the North." In any case, Althusius's ideal of a consociational commonwealth stands atop an older, broader body of Calvinian political reflection and lays out much of what Kuyper himself espoused. Althusius envisioned society as a hierarchy of voluntary associations, each warranted but also bound by the natural impulse that called it into being. Sovereignty lies in the commonwealth or the people as a whole but is distributed across its many components and domains, thus keeping responsibility as close as possible to the level of interest and competency, while at the same time avoiding both Bodin's unitary sovereignty, which was friendly to absolute monarchs, and mere majoritarian rule, which was the bane of democracy. Membership in the polity on this account inheres not in persons taken individually but as they belong to various groups, and the groups

14. Abraham Kuyper, "Sphere Sovereignty" [ET of *Souvereiniteit in Eigen Kring* (Amsterdam: J. H. Kruyt, 1880)], quotations, 467–68; historical narrative, 466–72.

15. On Althusius, see the edition of his *Politics* (Boston: Beacon Press, 1964), especially the introduction by its translator, Frederick S. Carney, and the preface by Carl J. Friedrich; also see the abridged edition (Indianapolis: Liberty Fund, 1994), with essays by Carney and Daniel J. Elazar.

constitute the components of the next higher level in the hierarchy of human association. Thus, persons make up the family, families—along with primary craft, trade, and other vocational associations—the town, towns the province, provinces the nation, nations the (Holy Roman) empire, and empires the world. Kuyper updated the model by proposing that the upper chambers of the Netherlands' provincial and national parliaments be elected by such associational groups—so many seats for labor, for business, for industry, for academia, and so forth. Kuyper's fear of individualism and of concentrated power, of both disorderly masses and unchecked elites, thus had direct precedent in early Reformed commonwealth thought and provided him with models to imagine a creative and energetic, yet controlled and responsible society under the conditions of modern life.

Two challenges beside the encroaching state arose to that model in Kuyper's lifetime and remain particularly vexing to our own. The one was imperialism, which was about to explode as Kuyper delivered his "Sphere Sovereignty" address and which would, over the next thirty years, bring the various European nations into a competitive scramble for domination in Asia and Africa, a race that reverberated back home with catastrophic results in Kuyper's last years. The other was "the social question"—the reality of poverty and powerlessness and the specter of class conflict—that arose under conditions of industrial capitalism.

On empire, Kuyper had to speak with mixed voice. The glory of the Dutch golden age was both symbolized and paid for by the fruits of the Dutch seaborne empire, and Kuyper covered over—actually, did not look closely for—its depredations with invocations of Calvinism. On the other hand, he denounced both the "cultivation" and the free-market systems that successive Dutch regimes had unleashed upon the East Indies in the nineteenth century to the great benefit of the Dutch exchequer but to the gross exploitation of the native peoples. If the Antirevolutionaries' colonial policy practiced its own, cultural form of imperialism—endorsing more vigorous government support of Christian evangelistic and educational ventures there—it at least put the indigenous people's holistic well-being as high as the Netherlands' economic interests as the relevant criterion for measuring such policy, and independence as the ultimate goal.[16]

South Africa was a different story, one of Dutch neglect and British highhandedness. Actually, Kuyper showed little interest in or respect for the Boers

16. See the section on colonial policy in Kuyper's *Ons Program* (Amsterdam: J. H. Kruyt, 1879). Kossmann treats the evolution of Dutch colonial policy in *Low Countries*, 163–64, 267–73, 398–412.

until their successful defiance of British claims in 1881, but thereafter he converted them into a model of Calvinist common-folk resistance for his own followers at home. The "coloured" population he had to pass over in embarrassed silence; the black majority he now casually derided as innately inferior, now limned as predators waiting to exploit the British-Boer internecine fighting. If we can block out such standard, if accentuated, racism of the times, we can appreciate how the South African situation stood for Kuyper as a pivotal test case of the rights of the weak for protection against the strong. Britain's continued and finally victorious imperial assault turned Kuyper permanently away from his once-vibrant Anglophilia and raised in his eyes the specter of ruthless materialistic philosophy, justified by the distorted biology of Darwin, now coming to rule international affairs. The fault in the present case, Kuyper said, lay with the turn of British policy away from the Christian Liberalism of Gladstone to the arrogant jingoism of Joseph Chamberlain; the end result, he predicted with no little accuracy, would be a conflagration of nations which, by extending British policy, would come around to destroy the British Empire. Put positively, Kuyper stood resolutely for international law, ceaselessly defended the rights of small nations to continued sovereignty and respect, and based these in the pluralistic ontology that raised diversity and free-forming action to divinely prescribed principles. Any human empire represented greed and pride, must proceed by subjugation and oppression, and would end in self-destruction. He not only anticipated that of the British Empire but also warned of it respecting the United States while touring there in 1898, the year American empire took a giant stride overseas. Thereafter, he reversed his previous practice and endorsed Democratic candidates for the U.S. presidency for their anti-imperial/peace platform, and sided with the Central Powers in World War I.[17]

Economic policy had never been the strong suit of Antirevolutionary leaders, who tended to subordinate it to what they took to be its foundations in and consequences for the public ethos. Kuyper long chided (classic) Liberal governments for being fixated on "merely material" goals to the neglect of "higher, moral" concerns. But this became a luxury he could less and less afford after 1875, when the Dutch economy along with the broader Atlantic world

17. Kuyper's attitudes toward South Africa are treated in detail in Chris A. J. van Koppen, *De Geuzen van de negentiende eeuw: Abraham Kuyper en Zuid-Afrika* (Wormer: Inmerc, 1992). See also R. Kuiper, *Zelfbeeld en wereldbeeld: antirevolutionairen en het buitenland, 1848–1905* (Kampen: Kok, 1992), which details Kuyper's hostility to British imperialism in North as well as South Africa in the early 1880s and his disappointment in American developments at the turn of the century. Kuyper's fullest statement, *The South African Crisis* (London: Stop the War Committee, 1900), appeared first in a French journal in 1900 and is reprinted in Bratt, *Abraham Kuyper*, 323–60.

passed from a quarter century of relatively easy expansion into much more constricted circumstances. The agrarian sector fell into a twenty-year depression; young Dutch industry slumped for a shorter period but, with its own ranks of the unemployed, obviously offered no home for the massive excess labor adrift in the countryside. This made the 1880s one of the Netherlands' hardest economic times in a century and forced Kuyper into some new considerations. He had alluded to working-class sufferings already in his pastorates and during his 1874–1876 term in the States General, but now he issued extensive statements in an 1889 newspaper series on manual labor and in his stirring address to open the Christian Social Congress that Dutch Protestants convened in Amsterdam in 1891, soon after the release of Pope Leo XIII's encyclical *Rerum Novarum*.[18]

Anyone who assumes an automatic affinity between conservative Protestantism and what passes today for "conservative" economic policy will be bewildered by Kuyper's position. With intense and often heated rhetoric he denounced laissez-faire, free-market economics as the spawn of "Revolution," as inimical to human well-being, material or spiritual, and as out of tune with Scripture and contrary to the will of God. The "Revolution" Kuyper named here is the French, but it could just as well have been the "Industrial," for the principles behind and the attitudes generated out of it constitute the deeper revolution in consciousness that Antirevolutionaries had always faulted most. Wherein did this revolution lie for economics? In replacing the spirit of "Christian compassion" with "the egoism of a passionate struggle for possessions." In the abrogation of the claims of community for the sake of sovereign individualism. In the commodification of labor, which denied the image of God and the rightful claims of a brother. In the idolization of the supposedly free market, which deprived the weak of their necessary protections, licensed the strong in their callous manipulations, and proclaimed the result to be the inevitable workings of nature. In the advertising that inculcated a "feverish desire for pleasure" and so established covetous consumerism as the norm of human happiness. The French Revolution, but also—Kuyper repeated throughout his work—the "utilitarian," the "laissez-faire," and the "Manchester" schools, which exfoliated the values of the Industrial Revolution,

> made the possession of money the highest good, and then, in the struggle for money, it set every man against every other. . . . As soon as that evil demon was unchained at the turn of the [nineteenth] century, no consideration was shrewd enough, no strategy crafty enough,

18. For data on the speech, see Kuyper, *Problem of Poverty*. Kuyper's newspaper series was published as *Handenarbeid* (Amsterdam: Wormser, 1889), and is available in English translation as "Manual Labor," in Bratt, *Abraham Kuyper*, 231–54.

> no deception outrageous enough among those who, through superiority of knowledge, position, and capital, took money—and ever more money—from the socially weaker.[19]

And since "it cannot be said often enough," as Kuyper intoned in his "Sphere Sovereignty" address, "that money creates power," the new bourgeoisie soon took control of the state, turning it into an agency of their own interests and annulling its divine mandate to protect the weak.[20]

That very fact, in Kuyper's eyes, mitigated progressive proposals to correct the abuses of industrial capitalism through legislative and regulatory reforms. "The stronger, almost without exception, have always known how to bend every custom and magisterial ordinance so that the profit is theirs and the loss belongs to the weaker." Specific changes might be legitimate: governments may alter inheritance laws to protect the poor, or (here Kuyper broke with his party's and nation's historic free trade policy) impose tariffs to protect domestic producers, or restrict free movement across borders to protect labor. But besides being prone to cooptation or to the state's imperial designs, Kuyper said, such gestures amounted to calling upon the physician when an architect was really needed. That is, "we must courageously and openly acknowledge that the Social Democrats are right" to insist that "the evil. . . [resides] in the *entire structure* of our social system." Socialists were wrong in the blueprint they drew up, he hastened to add, but even there, not so much for the details of its rooms as for neglecting to lay the foundations of the house in God's eternal ordinances. Kuyper repeated, and repeated again, that these broad principles were laid out along "clearly visible lines" in Scripture and creation, as if by repeating the insistence, the conflict within his own movement over how those ordinances applied to the current situation might go away.[21] But since the long conversation about Calvinism and economics has returned ultimately to its "ethic" vis-à-vis the "spirit" of capitalism, let us conclude with what Kuyper deemed these controlling principles to be and how they might pertain to our current situation.

First, Kuyper asserted a preferential option for the poor. Jesus, "just as his prophets before him and his apostles after him, invariably took sides *against* those who were powerful and living in luxury, and for the poor and oppressed." Granted, the poor are no better than the rich, he said, but Christ and Scripture always reprove their sins more gently than those of the wealthy.[22] Second, the merit of any economic system, both in its theory and in its practices, must

19. Kuyper, *Problem of Poverty*, 44–47.
20. Kuyper, "Sphere Sovereignty," 478.
21. Kuyper, *Problem of Poverty*, 33, 68; Kuyper, "Manual Labor," 235.
22. Kuyper, *Problem of Poverty*, 62; see also 35–42, 60–63.

be measured by the respect it exercises for human beings as bearers of the image of God and by the basic security it provides for human existence. Reducing the laborer to a "factor of production" violates her dignity and the divinely mandated use of her God-given creative powers, which properly make work an opportunity and a blessing. Third, mutuality or solidarity is the biblical ideal for human society and no less the pragmatic grounds for its true flourishing. God created human beings to live relationally—with each other, with the nonhuman order, as well as with and underneath the cover of God's transcendent person. Practically, this obviates any theory or system that proceeds from or to the individual person as isolate or sovereign. It obviates as well any proposal that looks to the triumph or eradication of a particular group or class, or that maximizes (whether as means, end, or inevitable consequence) the separation or perpetual antagonism of peoples. Kuyper's is first to last a communal theory with a communal ethic—in particular, giving property rights derivative, not primary, standing and assuming that people together can both understand and competently modify market operations.[23]

But Kuyper was also sensitive to the realities of power and neither expected nor desired that these be rendered inoperative. Rather, he looked to the division and balancing of powers, in society and economics as well as government, for the best approximation of justice and equity that might be attained on this earth. Thus, his answer to "the social question" of the time was to empower labor through collective organization, self-initiated but state protected, so that it might register its due weight in the struggles and negotiations of economic life. This would reduce not only the oppression but also the demoralization of workers, he thought, by forging solidarity with their fellows. A chain of labor councils, arrayed in a series of concentric spheres, starting from the local grass roots and extending upward and outward over the entire nation, would far more likely be responsive to workers' own interests and expertise than would state regulators. The proper role for government would be to supervise the binding arbitration whereby labor and capital resolved any outstanding disputes. This empowerment also required a political basis, Kuyper added. Democratizing the franchise would ensure as nothing else could the representation of worker needs in the halls of legislation and cement workers' solidarity with the rest of the nation.[24]

"Above" such practical arrangements lay the most important set of considerations, namely, the "moral" domain of (collective) "consciousness": "Because we are conscious beings, almost everything depends on the standard of values which

23. Kuyper lays out his general principles of diagnosis and remedy in *Problem of Poverty*, 30–34, 50–52, 59–79.

24. Kuyper elaborates these measures in "Manual Labor."

our consciousness constructs."[25] Kuyper's rhetoric on this score might be taken as dispensing the opiate of the masses, as when he notes how the pious poor are more content with little than the impious, but such statements read in context are warnings to wealthy agnostics about the price of their derision of religion. A proper social consciousness, he argued, would displace materialism, control, and egotism with justice, equity, and compassion as primary values, as the spontaneous or default criteria by which people judged policy and behavior. Kuyper assigned the cultivation of such values to church, school, and press (read "media"), the organs of public opinion, since the state was incompetent and the market uninterested in generating them. But ethos depended on more than ethics, he knew. Workers' morality was closely tied to their morale, which in turn was grounded in their own sense of their life chances. Here Kuyper's prescription was definitively petit bourgeois: the channeling of sexual desire within marriage and family relations; the availability of reliable, dignified work; and a minimal dependence on welfare subsidies. Each of these would feed back into the other to build energetic, disciplined citizens who upheld their own part while contributing to the public interest that surmounted their own individual interest.[26]

Thus, Kuyper's voice sounds some perennial tones of Calvinist social thinking: the concern with whole integrated systems, with the distribution and balance of powers so as to control the aggression that is the prime collective expression of human depravity, the uneasy regard for wealth as a proving ground rather than any proof of salvation. Kuyper's distinctive contribution to this tradition might be defined as a constellation made up of vigorous localism, praise of diversity, pluralism as a principle, and democracy as a positive step rather than reluctant concession, all arrayed under the rubric of sphere sovereignty. That contribution might have new relevance as we consider that today not the state but the market has become the "sphere of spheres" intruding on all others, needing sharp checks from government and communal consciousness alike;[27] that globalization threatens uniformity but also makes possible new departures in creative cultural expression; and that empowering the commons on the local level has no small part in preventing abuse by all the powers, whether these be the market, the magistrate, or the American imperium.

25. Kuyper, *Problem of Poverty*, 73.

26. Ibid., 68–75.

27. Since "sphere encroachment" is such a basic principle in Kuyperian thought, it is especially illuminating to read Michael Walzer's classic *Spheres of Justice: A Defense of Pluralism and Equality* (New York: Basic Books, 1983), as well as the more recent entries by Thomas Frank, *One Market under God: Extreme Capitalism, Market Populism, and the End of Economic Democracy* (New York: Doubleday, 2000), and Robert Kuttner, *Everything for Sale: The Virtues and Limits of Markets* (New York: Knopf, 1997).

7

Calvin and Reformed Social Thought in Latin America

Eduardo Galasso Faria

My theme starts from the assumption, recognized by some authors, that Protestant thought in Latin America since the nineteenth century has had as its matrix the Calvinist doctrinal accents of the Presbyterian churches in the United States. It is my intention to demonstrate how the American Presbyterian missionary vector in the nineteenth century, which was fundamental in shaping Latin American Protestantism, was rooted in deviations from Calvin's thought which were current since seventeenth-century Calvinism, but that it recovered in large part its "Calvinian" identity in the twentieth century. This recovery, associated with the development of ecumenical ideas in Latin America, started with the Panama Congress (1916) and reached its climax in the 1960s—ironically, through the same vector of American Presbyterian mission.

I will proceed by briefly sketching the emergence of Protestantism in Latin America, then by describing the various theological strains that American missionaries brought with them in the nineteenth century, and finally by analyzing how a Calvinian emphasis was recovered under an initiative begun by Richard Shaull in the 1950s.

The first Protestant presence in Latin America dates from the sixteenth century with the French expedition of Villegaignon (1555–1560), which had been prepared with Coligny's support to establish a colony (Antarctic France) in Rio de Janeiro. The Huguenots were looking for a refuge where they could live and worship faithfully and freely. John Calvin took a personal interest in the enterprise and sent pastors to establish the first Protestant church in

America according to Genevan form. Its first worship service was held in Rio de Janeiro on March 10, 1557.

During the seventeenth century, Dutch merchants who were trying to expand their sugar trade occupied the northeast area of Brazil and started a Reformed church on the Genevan model there too. They organized the first Reformed synod in Brazil. Their pastoral presence was significant, especially among the Indians. Another attempt at French settlement was made at Maranhão in the north of the country—Equinotical France—from 1641 to 1644. However, faced by firm Portuguese resistance, this Reformed community was unable to establish itself in this Roman Catholic dominion.

After the Commerce and Navigation Treaty signed by Portugal and England in 1810, which guaranteed religious liberty for English people and others, a regular flow of Protestants began to arrive in Brazil. By 1840, they were coming to countries under Spanish control as well. Thus, "immigration Protestantism" preceded "mission Protestantism." The first of the Protestant missionaries were Anglican churchmen who came to Brazil. They were followed by Lutherans (1824), Methodists (1835), Congregationalists (1855), Presbyterians (1859), and Baptists (1871).

MISSION PROTESTANTISM

Thus, it was in the second half of the nineteenth century and in the form of "mission Protestantism" that a more enduring and significant Reformed presence took root in Latin America. In forty years American Presbyterians sent more than forty missionaries to Brazil, and their following grew more than those of the other denominations. In 1891 the Presbyterians numbered fifty churches, thirty-one pastors, and two schools.[1] Thus, the Protestantism that is so diverse today had Reformed Calvinist thought as its formative matrix. In that matrix two types of agent soon appeared: first, evangelists who organized churches, and then educators who in 1870 founded the São Paulo American School, now Mackenzie Presbyterian University.

The missions, supported by liberal Latin American politicians, grew up in the ideological context of Manifest Destiny, which dreamed of extending the American way of life, culture, and religion to the whole world. Over the course of the nineteenth century, England's hegemonic position over Latin America was replaced by that of the United States, which took control in the name of the Monroe Doctrine. This influence resulted in the preponderance of liberal

1. Antonio Gouvêa Mendonça, *O Celeste Porvir*, Inserção do Protestantismo no Brasil (São Paulo: IMS, Pendão Real, Aste, 1995), 32.

modernity over the conservative Roman Catholic Church. The objective was to transform Latin American societies by preparing modern and liberal citizens. Overall, American missionary action in the area of religion and education supported American political and economic expansionism. The mission enterprise as a whole represented a mix of Protestantism with the liberal ideal of modernization.

These objectives were nevertheless not achieved. Despite having 100,000 followers by the end of the nineteenth century, the Protestant missions and their theology could not keep pace with the transformations occurring in Brazilian society. Protestantism had to seek refuge in its particular *religious* vision of faith, unable to participate in the important "autonomous re-creation"[2] of history at that moment. The political change in Brazil from monarchy to republic thus was made under the influence of Auguste Comte's positivism, not under the influence of the Presbyterian and Reformed churches.

Few historians recognize a meaningful Protestant presence in Latin American society today; many even describe it as a "rare and exotic phenomenon." Why did Protestantism in the course of its development lose its initial "utopic possibilities" (Rubem Alves) of transformation in Latin America? The question leads us back to an analysis of the new configuration articulated by American Presbyterian religious thinking in the nineteenth century. This Protestantism was highly subjective and individualistic, focused on sanctification and salvation, and was thus not able to stimulate in Latin American society a structural understanding of its problems.

Put another way, while church historians recognize that Presbyterian bodies remained followers of Calvin in their system of ecclesiastical government, the same was not true with respect to Calvin's theological ideas. Thus, it is not a mistake to say, as did Dietrich Bonhoeffer of the United States, that Latin American Protestantism is a Protestantism without Reformation. To cite an indigenous authority, Antonio Mendonça says that Reformed theology in Brazil was inconsistent from the outset, maintaining one form of teaching in the seminaries and another in the pulpit.

PRINCETON THEOLOGY

Beyond the Puritan type of Protestant theology that had prevailed in the United States since the time of colonization, certain other strains were introduced in the training of the missionaries who came to Latin America. As a

2. José Bittencourt Filho, *Matriz Religiosa Brasileira*, Religiosidade e Mudança Social (Petrópolis: Vozes, Koinonia, 2003), 125.

result, these missionaries received little of John Calvin but much of the Calvinist orthodoxy that marked Presbyterian thinking in seventeenth-century Europe and that was taken up in the United States by the Princeton theology. This school of Protestant thought adopted Thomas Reid's Scottish common sense realism with the objective of defending the Christian faith against Deism. The starting point of Reid's theory was that the common people using their ordinary senses with the methods of the natural sciences could directly ascertain the truth based on facts and intuition. The formulations of this theology, starting from an objective analysis of the Bible, transformed faith into a practical and intellectualist matter.

In reaction against this sterile, rigid, and discouraging type of orthodoxy, there appeared in the second half of the nineteenth century, fed by Pietism and apocalyptic ideas, discussions about the millennium and the end times.[3] The transformation of society by church action, the premillennialists taught, would occur only after the millennium that commenced with the return of Christ. The renewed pouring out of the Spirit, victory over the Antichrist, and the proclamation of the gospel worldwide would carry civilization to progress and a new age of peace, justice, and prosperity.

Premillennialism prevailed on the evangelical side of American Protestantism, sustaining the idea that the second coming of Christ would occur before the establishment of his kingdom. Any postmillennial idea about improving society through the social gospel was forsaken. Premillennialist missionary work aimed at salvation for unbelievers individually, bringing them to conversion before Christ's return. If postmillennialism aimed to establish an educational system to Christianize society, premillennialism hoped for a divine intervention in history to bring everything to consummation.

REVIVAL THEOLOGY

Beside this intellectualist stream of orthodoxy, a Pietist current was simultaneously developing, built on religious experience grounded in the emotions. While the old and elitist Calvinism with its emphasis on predestination continued to stress human disability and the election of a few, the revival theology of the nineteenth century pointed instead to free will and the love of God, which offered salvation to all. Charles Finney's (1792–1875) perfectionism announced the possibility of the abandonment of sin by man and the acceptance of everybody by Christ. This preaching called for personal sanctification that, being multiplied, would grow into an effort to establish the kingdom of God on earth and build a

3. Mendonça, *O Celeste Porvir*, 67.

better world. Social issues such as poverty, the abolition of slavery, and the moralization of society were among its themes, as subordinate elements.

At the end of the nineteenth century, with the development of the Wesleyan holiness idea of sanctification, a "great inversion" occurred.[4] "Revival *and* reform" became "evangelization *or* reform." The practice of holiness put ideas about building the kingdom and the social gospel on a secondary level, giving place to dispensationalism (J. N. Darby and C. I. Scofield) and amplifying the gospel's distance from ongoing historical events.

The American Presbyterian churches that were active in Latin American missions saw social gospel ideas as dangerous. Old School Presbyterians in the South, basing their arguments on the Scriptures, defended slavery as a natural human condition (J. H. Thornwell, 1812–1862). In the North, the heirs of Charles Hodge warned that the social gospel denied traditional doctrines and reduced the kingdom of God to its material and worldly heretical expression, as was evidenced by what was happening in theological liberalism and New England theology.

The fundamentalism that emerged out of the convergence of Old School Presbyterian theology and dispensational premillennialism played an important role in Latin American Protestantism. Its origin lay in opposition to liberalism, scientific advances, and secularism. It posited Scripture as the infallible ground for the affirmation of the supernatural world in the same manner as nature provided the source of mundane knowledge. The authority of the Bible was derived from its inspiration, which makes the infallibility of the text the warranty against difficult problems with science. Fundamentalism made grounding doctrine firmly, without doubts, of first importance.

This summary, although fragmentary, is very important to understanding the Latin American Protestantism that grew out of American missionary ideas. By the end of the nineteenth century, the Presbyterian churches, together with other mainstream churches, manifested a Puritan faith marked by an exemplary family life, discipline, economy, cleanliness, honesty, and the rejection of addictions, together with Pietist and premillennialist ideas that left it without the perspective needed to face social and political problems.

The churches' school system, which followed American patterns, brought innovations in pedagogical methods, female teachers, mixed classes, physical education, and discipline. The liturgy in the churches was very simple and informal. The preaching was doctrinal, with a moralist, monitory, and apologetic character, especially against the Roman Catholic Church, which was viewed as non-Christian.

4. José Míguez Bonino, *Rostros del Protestantismo Latinoamericano* (Buenos Aires: Nueva Creacion, 1995), 40.

In the twentieth century, after the First World War and especially in the 1930s, many changes appeared in Latin American Protestantism that significantly increased the number of missionaries that followed the line of holiness, premillennialist, and fundamentalist movements coming from Great Britain and the United States. After the Second World War, a new wave of these missionaries, influencing the mainstream churches, affirmed again "an ethic of separation from the world together with rigorous legalism" that was linked more and more with the middle classes.[5] They saw political and social action as unacceptable or at least as nonreligious. They rejected communism, socialism, and any other leftist position. Their political concern was limited to supporting liberal parties that would maintain the freedom to preach, as opposed to clerical and conservative groups. According to Míguez Bonino, there was great admiration for the democracy of the United States, anticommunism, and fundamentalism. The rightist positions were attractive because of their "military promises of moral order and stability."[6]

THE ECUMENICAL MOVEMENT

On the other hand, already at the Panama Congress (1916), signs of change and modernization were emerging in Latin American Protestantism, including new possibilities of political and social action as means of bearing Christian witness. In Brazil an ecumenical current developed under the leadership of Presbyterian pastors Erasmo Braga and Epaminondas Mello do Amaral, as did another current, opposed to ecumenical approaches, under Eduardo Carlos Pereira and Álvaro Reis. Ecumenical leaders were engaged with dreams about the "possibility of mutual cooperation with Roman Catholics to have a real Christianization of Latin America."[7]

The Montevideo Congress (1925) emphasized both the social aspects of democracy and the message of the social gospel, insisting that issues related to fair conditions for workers, health, honest salaries, and education were very important for the churches—in other words, urging a "practical and nondogmatic gospel."[8] The Congress of Havana (1929) proposed to make Protestantism a *Latin* reality, against its identification with American imperialism.

5. Ibid.
6. Ibid.
7. Antonio Gouvêa Mendonça, "A Herança e a Contribuição Reformada no Brasil," *Revista do Seminário Teológico de São Paulo* 36 (1985): 33.
8. Juan-José Tamayo and Juan Bosh, eds., *Panorama de la Teologia Latinoamericana* (Navarra: Editorial Verbo Divino, 2001), 59.

There was also an effort to abandon the spirit of controversy with the Roman Catholic Church.

The 1929 world crisis made evident the growing misery of the people as well as the disaster of free-market liberalism. This had significant consequences for Protestantism. One was the upsurge of evangelical Protestantism, marked by Pietism and Puritanism and influenced by the heritage of the Great Awakenings in the United States (Jonathan Edwards, Charles Finney, Dwight L. Moody), but without links to the progressive emphasis of the Panama Congress. Here conversion to Christ was said to have nothing to do with politics; rather, the purpose of this movement was to reproduce American ecclesiastical models, with separate churches growing numerically. Enemies were the social gospel (modernism) and the Roman Catholic Church (the Antichrist).

In the 1960s populism suffered a fall (Brazil, 1964; Argentina, 1966), economic development theory was abandoned, and a new alliance between the bourgeoisie, American corporations, and military groups influenced civil governments. The consequence was the growth of revolutionary movements, as in Cuba in the 1950s. Against this new revolutionary wave, governments planned serious repression against popular groups and workers.

The United States responded with the national security doctrine for Latin America. Its main point was the idea of a global war by the Western world against international communism and subversion. The army, not civil forces, was deemed the nation's moral support, even though it repressed individual rights.

RICHARD SHAULL: CHURCH AND SOCIETY

At this historical moment a new discussion emerged in Latin American Protestantism about the relation between church and society, the mission of the church, and social ethics. On the one hand stood the ecumenical movement, represented by the Latin American Protestant Commission for Christian Education (CELADEC), Church and Society in Latin America (ISAL), the Latin American Union of Evangelical Youth (ULAJE), and the Ecumenical Center of Documentation and Information (CEDI), linked with the World Council of Churches. On the other stood the evangelical movement, including the Biblical Student Alliance (ABU), World Vision, and National Vision of Evangelization, all linked to the 1923 International Congress of World Evangelization and the 1974 congress of the same name in Lausanne.

New ideas about the church and its mission began to appear in Latin America in general and in Brazilian Protestantism in particular during the 1950s. As a result, Protestant youth developed a critical posture in relation to mainstream churches and called for "a new relationship between Church and society, Evangelicals and ecumenicals, beyond ideological and theological questions," favoring a renewal in ecclesiology.[9]

At this point, prominence must be given to the role of the American Presbyterian missionary Richard Shaull, who has left a deep mark on Latin American Protestant thinking. As a youth leader and professor at a theological seminary, he initiated intensive reflections about historical events that began with the Reformed faith and John Calvin's thought.

Shaull's presence in the Campinas Presbyterian Seminary (1952–1959) was preceded by ten years as an evangelist and pastor in Colombia. With his church and a Roman Catholic group, he started a health and literacy project there, going to live with his family in a slum in the city of Barranquilla.

He tried to incite young people to participate in politics as a Christian vocation for the transformation of society. It was here that he first came into contact with Marxist students, who challenged him to understand why it was the Marxists and not the Christians (who were moralist and Pietist) that were engaged in the struggle for the transformation of Colombian society and concerned for the place of the poor within it. He challenged the people of the church to participate in union movements, which led to dissensions among them. He denounced violations of human rights. When the situation became dangerous, he went into hiding and was unable to return and continue his work.

The challenges in Colombia prepared Shaull for studies on Marxism at Union Theological Seminary in New York City. After taking his doctorate at Princeton with Paul Lehmann, he understood the relation of his faith to revolutionary action in a new way, liberating himself to act ethically outside the church, free from "the cumbersome obstruction of traditional ecclesiology."[10] He discerned that at the center of revolution and humanization it was possible to understand the political character of divine activity in building a new humanity.

The political situation in Brazil gave rise to nationalist and anti-imperialist movements, including important action by the trade unions and mass agitation. With the victory of Fidel Castro's revolution—very attractive to leftist political figures—dreams of reformist development were smashed and altered by revolutionary ideas. Shaull thought about the meaningful opportunity this historical context offered the church to influence the situation. The old moral, Puritan heritage with its negative, irrelevant precepts widened the believer's

9. Luiz Longuini Neto, *O Novo Rosto da Missão* (Viçosa: Ultimato, 2002), 282.

10. Richard Shaull and Barbara Hall, "Reflections from Somewhere along the Road," *Theology Today* 29, no. 1 (1973): 3.

separation from the world. Latin American Protestant churches, linked to the middle classes, had no attraction for the poor. On the other hand, Roman Catholics were living a moment of renewal, spurred by interest in social problems. Would it be possible for Protestants to work with Roman Catholics free from any spirit of controversy?

It was necessary to prepare the church for a new moment. At Campinas Seminary, Shaull intended to prepare pastors to contribute to the transformation of society. He tried to change the emphasis of theological thinking from the old orthodoxy of Hodge and Strong to the dialectical school of Barth and Brunner. The seminarians needed to be taken out of their ghetto and put into contact with rural and urban society and the world of politics. It was important to break with the attraction of a bourgeois life of security and prestige to fight for a church structure ready to accomplish its mission in the world.

In class Shaull challenged the seminarians to practice what they were discussing about mission; this was possible in a distant industrial quarter. Shaull also began to participate in the national congresses of Protestant youth, speaking about Christians and politics, politics and revolution, and so forth. This resulted in the little book (published first in Portuguese and afterward in Spanish) *Christianity and the Social Revolution* (1953), which addressed the challenges that communism posed for Christians.

With the Christian university students in the UCEB (Christian Students Union of Brazil)—itself part of the World Student Christian Movement (WSCM)—Shaull studied the means for them to make a distinctive contribution to the political moment. In their unique position, which was different from that of Marxists and of Roman Catholics, Protestant university students could participate in Jesus Christ's promise for the human condition without being constrained by a model of a perfect society ("This kind of thinking always leads to the absolutization of ideology and of the political party").[11] When students argued with him about the inadequacy of Barthian theology as an instrument for political action, Shaull answered with a quotation from Bonhoeffer: with respect to the established order, the Christian can die to the past and expect new possibilities.

He encouraged work in the slums and at Vila Anastácio, a workers' quarter in São Paulo, where he organized a project (1957–1958) in which seminarians and laypeople worked incognito in the factories to understand the mission of the church there. It was the first experiment of this kind in Latin America.

11. Richard Shaull, "Entre Jesus and Marx: Reflexóes Sobre os a nos que passei no Brasil," in *De Dentro do Furacão: Richard Shaull e os Primórdios da Teologia da Libertação* (São Paulo: Sagarana Editora, 1985), 203.

ISAL: CHURCH AND SOCIETY IN LATIN AMERICA

Shaull made another important contribution through the organization Church and Society in Latin America (ISAL). While preparing for its Evanston Assembly (1954), the World Council of Churches (WCC) decided to organize studies on Christian social responsibility in areas undergoing rapid transformation in Latin America, and Shaull was invited to participate. Following that, in Rio de Janeiro in 1955, the Sector of Social Responsibility was organized within the Brazilian ecumenical organization, the Evangelical Confederation of Brazil (CEB). The historical moment that Brazil was living through and the relation it could have with the Christian faith was studied in different meetings: Social Transformations in Brazil, 1956; The Presence of the Church in the Evolution of Nationality, 1960; Christ and the Revolutionary Process in Brazil, 1962. This last meeting took place in the city of Recife, in the northeast of Brazil, the poorest region of the country, and the matters under discussion included revolution and the kingdom of God, prophets in a time of social and political transformation, and the mission of the church in a society in crisis. There was significant participation by important personalities of the country, including the economist Celso Furtado.

The Sector of Social Responsibility was closed after the military coup in 1964, which led to a heavy persecution of progressive groups. All its material was destroyed, and pastors collaborating with it were denounced by other pastors. Some had to flee. Shaull was forbidden to return to Brazil for a period of twenty years. Many people in the country were tortured and killed. Among them were many Christians. Paul Stuart Wright, a Brazilian politician, Presbyterian presbyter, and son of an American missionary, was murdered in 1972. The same happened in Argentina to Maurício Lopez and to the Colombian priest Camilo Torres and many others. While the group that had collaborated in ISAL was weakened, Latin America began to receive a large number of American fundamentalist missionaries.

The high point in the era of political involvement and discussion on Christian social ethics was reached when Richard Shaull spoke at the World Conference of Church and Society in Geneva in 1966. He opened the way to a new and radical orientation of the churches in relation to the modern world, "pressing them to the centre of the revolution" (Gaughan Hinton). In the face of the persistent economic and political problems of the Third World, it was necessary to change the emphasis spelled out by the first WCC assembly in Amsterdam in 1948—to create a responsible society in a position between liberalism and communism. By 1966, as Paul Albrecht wrote, "the world situation compelled the Churches to adopt a new and radical ecumenical testimony in favor of justice, grounded in the Revolution Theology of Richard Shaull."[12] For Shaull it was necessary to understand the pressure against any attempt at social transformation that came from technological advances. It was important to understand that the established order could not be transformed without a profound revolutionary process for the humanization of society.

It is impossible to understand the renewal of Latin American Protestant thinking without knowing more about ISAL itself. ISAL was organized in 1961 with the assistance of the WCC and the participation of Luis Odell, Julio de Santa Ana, and many other lay Christian theologians and sociologists from Argentina, Bolivia, Brazil, Uruguay, and other countries. Its purpose was to work on questions of faith and participation in the Latin American historical situation. Its first conference took place in Huampaní, Peru, in 1961, and was devoted to studying the responsibility of the Protestant church amid social change. In reality this provided "the first opportunity to be conscious of the profound meaning of the Latin American revolution."[13]

In the beginning, the mainstream Latin American churches could understand and carry forward ISAL's emphasis on the church's public responsibility and its testimony to Christ's redemption of the whole person, that is, the possibility his incarnation held to make possible a fully human life. The most important fact in the history of ISAL's official deliberations about the church's relation to society (1961, Huampaní; 1966, El Tabo; 1967, Montevideo; 1971, Ñaña), according to Míguez Bonino, was the commitment to preserve the transcendence of the gospel amid the church's historical involvement. ISAL's first consultation did not make clear the distinction between revolution and development, but at the second, in 1966 in Chile, the initial idea of reformism was abandoned. The meeting concluded that it was impossible to achieve development through technology; the way had to proceed through revolution, supported by a historical and contextual theology (Richard Shaull and Paul Lehmann) with an opening to socialism in the revolutionary process, always looking for the signs of the times.

ISAL, without the participation and sympathy of the ecclesiastical institutions, tried to understand the Latin American historical situation starting from a Marxist analysis and liberation theology. In the 1970s, after the WCC's Bangkok Conference (1972), discussion about mission in Latin America gave more and more attention to social concerns, owing to the particular prevalence

12. Paul Albrecht, "A situação do pensamento social cristão após a Guerra Fria," in *Contexto Pastoral* 2, no. 1 (1992): 4.

13. *America Hoy: Accion de Dios y responsabilidad del Hombre* (Montevideo: ISAL, 1966), 14.

of institutionalized violence there. The 1971 consultation in Ñaña planned to undertake the task of mobilizing the people in the churches, questioning the contradictions and lack of substance in the imported theological formulations, and trying to express its thinking with formulations that would spring from the struggle of the people as a revolution on the march—not systematic or abstract but fed by its own dynamic. On its tenth anniversary, ISAL published *Christianity and Society*, which defended Christian testimony in the face of the social problem in an ecumenical spirit.

One observer concluded that ISAL made possible in Latin America "a new pastoral and missiological posture for the Churches" along the lines of ecumenism, ecclesiology, and interdisciplinarity.[14] Sometimes it was criticized for lacking a healthy balance between its activism and a more mystical spirituality. In any event, it made possible an autonomous Protestant thinking distinct from the practice of the American churches and expressing a Christian testimony in the difficult economic, social, and political situation of Latin America in the second half of the twentieth century. It influenced what missionaries offered in Latin America, changing their message from individual salvation to social witness in the historical context of poverty and corruption.

RECOVERING CALVIN

One of Shaull's important lessons to his students was his concern with the recovery of Calvin's image. In academic contexts Calvin was known as authoritarian, implacable, intolerant, dogmatic, and particularly associated with the origin of capitalism. In the Presbyterian context his thinking was identified with the formulations of the Westminster Confession of Faith and the "Five Points of Calvinism" (Total depravity, Unconditional election, Limited atonement, Irresistible grace, Perseverance of the saints—TULIP) from the Synod of Dort (1618–1619).

For Brazilian Presbyterians, Calvin's ideas were identified mainly with the doctrines of total depravity and double predestination. According to Shaull, the importance of restoring an interest in Calvin's thinking was to cultivate a faith that gave direction to a Christian way of living, and not only to learn about the doctrines of a remote past. Calvin's inheritance was a living one when applied to the search for responses to new problems and situations.

This new vision of Calvin inspired Shaull to prepare a seminar on Calvin for the World Alliance of Reformed Churches conference in São Paulo in 1959. To support his argument about the importance of knowing Calvin and

14. Longuini Neto, *O Novo Rosto da Missão*, 144.

Calvinism, he introduced André Biéler's *La pensée économique et sociale de Calvin* (1959), pointing out the similarity between social transformations in the sixteenth and twentieth centuries. For him Calvin, sustaining the doctrine of the sovereignty of God in a time of uncertainty, spelled out what was probably the most important guideline for Latin America's future: "transforming the Gospel into a dynamic and creative force in the modern world."[15]

The important task was to study seriously all the works of Calvin in order to acquire "a perspective according to the central structure of his thinking."[16] Two distortions present in most Presbyterian churches had to be considered. One of them was the Protestant scholasticism that understood Christian faith as a system of doctrines to be accepted without reflection by the people. For Shaull, Calvin's theology had nothing to do with that. On the contrary, Calvin showed a vitality of thinking that made it possible to understand the great realities of Jesus Christ. The other distortion was Pietism, for which the purpose of studying theology was only to emphasize one's personal experience with Jesus. Forgetting the God who acts in history and the cosmic character of redemption, Pietism contributed to destroying the basis for Christian responsibility regarding the social and political problems of the world—as in a certain way Luther did.

In 1971 Shaull again took up the Calvinist inheritance, studying the Puritan revolution of 1648 in England and discovering its attraction for the "masterless men" who were not conformed to the society of the time.[17] Among many people who believed that things could not be changed, Calvinists spoke of the reality of the God who acts, remaking the world.

Shaull also criticized the Barthian perspective on Calvin, which did not explain the conditions of being a vanguard of the revolutionary cause but worked only as a conservative and non-transgressive force to think and change society. Recovering Calvin's inheritance could be a fundamental task to feed a new theology in the context of revolution in Latin America.

THE EVANGELICAL MOVEMENT

Meanwhile, Latin American Protestantism was growing stronger in the 1960s, especially the evangelical movement, which was initially intended to be a conservative alternative to the ecumenical movement and was shaped by groups

15. Richard Shaull, "Palestras em un Seminário sobre Calvinismo," in *Suplemento Teológico d' OCAOS* (Campinas: Seminário Presbiteriano de Campinas, 1960), 23.
16. Ibid.
17. Richard Shaull, "Igreja e Teologia na Voragem da Revolução," in *De Dentro do Furacão*, 121.

such as the Evangelical World Fellowship (EWF), World Vision, the School of Missions of Fuller Theological Seminary, and the magazine *Christianity Today*.

The Wheaton Congress (1966) was planned to be a reflection on mission in opposition to the ecumenical movement, to shift the emphasis from social action to evangelization. It also provided an opportunity to organize the Latin American Theological Fraternity (FTL) with many theologians from different denominations under the leadership of Samuel Escobar. Its aim was to provide an alternative to ISAL. As a result, divergences between evangelicals and American fundamentalists emerged, with the final decision being that only Latin Americans could be members of FTL.

Yet 1969, after the Latin American Congress of Evangelization (CLADE I, evangelical) and the Latin American Conference of Evangelization (CELA III, ecumenical), spelled a radicalization at a crucial moment in Latin American Protestant history, when the two movements "articulated an opening toward ecclesiological renewal in Latin America concerning the relations between Church and society, and bearing on establishing a new concept of missiological and pastoral practice for the Protestant Churches."[18]

FTL was reinforced by the Lausanne Alliance (1974) and reaffirmed a special relation between evangelization and political responsibilities. Its new purpose was to relate the gospel to Latin American culture and history. Orlando Costas and René Padilha were among the leaders supporting the Lausanne Alliance who were present in the Brazilian Congress of Evangelization at Belo Horizonte, in 1983, against the opposition of American fundamentalists such as Donald McGravan, Peter Wagner, and Richard Sturs, who considered them too progressive.

CONCLUSION

Since its effective implantation in Latin America in the second half of the nineteenth century, Protestantism has contained some options for missionary action in which the economic and social thinking of Calvin was present, sometimes indirectly, sometimes explicitly. As in England, Scotland, or the United States, there was evident concern to make the city of God clearly visible in the city of humanity. The universal nature of Calvin's purposes, which played an important role in the debates on Western democracy, was to be found among the continent's mainstream Protestant churches. They frequently formed alliances with Latin American political parties, supporting the struggle for liberal modernization.

18. Longuini Neto, *O Novo Rosto da Missão*, 11.

However, the theological ideas of Calvin suffered many changes in application and development as they migrated to other countries. The Protestant orthodoxy of the seventeenth century, characterized by doctrinaire and intellectual assertions, parted company with the living experience of the human relationship with God and its consequences for social concerns. This apologetical and reductionist vision created a repetitive theological discourse that claimed to be a precise doctrinal formulation, ready to denounce divergent forms of faith it considered heretical.

Further transformations came under ideas inspired by Pietism and revivalism, which had a considerable influence on the missionary movement in the United States. Although often walking side by side with a social emphasis, in the end this sort of evangelicalism opened the way to the great inversion described by Míguez Bonino, which offered the churches a false choice between evangelization and social reform. Along with Puritanism, these currents expressed some very subjective and negative ideas of salvation and sanctification, in association with millennialist and dispensationalist beliefs bereft of any historical concern whatsoever.

A theology limited to repeating the main scholastic doctrines linked with American culture and imperialism, strongly influenced by the ideology of Manifest Destiny, prevented Protestantism from focusing on a spirituality capable of cultivating a Latin American vision of structural problems in such a way as to act in an original and prophetic manner in society. It weakened the utopian vision and openings for transformation that had been apparent in Protestantism at the outset.

The Panama (1916) and Havana (1929) Congresses marked the recovery of a social gospel emphasis in dealing with issues such as education, health, working conditions, and fair wages in a manner linked to the proclamation of the gospel. But the suspicion against the social gospel and other liberal emphases strengthened the conservative and fundamentalist spirit of the new waves of missionaries to Latin America in the twentieth century, establishing a spirit of exclusivism and segregation for Protestants while raising difficulties for an authentic dialogue within their historical context. Later, an evangelical Protestantism developed with the objective of increasing the number of members of the Protestant churches, and so it concentrated on attacking the Roman Catholic Church and the social gospel movement. Meanwhile, on the Latin American political scene an alliance between the military, the bourgeoisie, and American capitalism promoted the repression of the people and of proletarian movements in their fight against harsh economic conditions.

The divergence between conservative and liberal positions in the 1960s was confirmed in the growth of the evangelical movement of the 1970s that was linked to Lausanne over against the ecumenical movements linked to the

WCC. In ecumenical Protestantism, starting from ISAL, the vision of a new and significant relationship between church and society in Latin America promised a breath of liberation through dreams and struggles for social and political transformation. This creative and prophetic movement based on Calvin's practice was quenched by the Brazilian military coup d'état, the influence of which spread to the whole of Latin America, resulting in a long and painful time of institutionalized violence.

It is easy to see throughout the history of Latin American Protestantism how the rivalries and the difficulties in overcoming differences made Christian action in a spirit of respect and unity almost impossible. The controversies about correct beliefs stressed differences, preventing a positive and sound understanding in which faith and testimony could be shared.

Today in Latin American Protestantism there are indications that a fraternal and more mature relationship may be possible among currents of thinking that were once divided mainly on the issue of Christian social and political action. A shared view is growing of mission as evangelization and political and social action all together, and favoring closer relations between conservative and ecumenical circles.

On the other hand, a great challenge is now arising from Pentecostal groups, who have often been discriminated against by other Christian groups. Some Protestant groups see Pentecostalism in a favorable light, offering an opening for a necessary and fruitful dialogue. Recently, during a preparatory meeting for the Ninth WCC Assembly in Brazil (Rio de Janeiro, 2005), Pentecostal representatives emphasized the need to destroy barriers and prejudices between "evangelical" Pentecostals and ecumenical Protestants. They said that there is no longer any polarization between their positions, but that they are complementary.

They have also declared that "growing in numbers presents some problems" and that there is a need to recover "beyond an individualist and futurist faith a serious prophetic dimension, committed to present day society." For their part, representatives of what may be called mainstream churches said that "it is necessary to overthrow prejudices against Pentecostals" in the search for "commitment and identification in relation to the social causes. . . . We cannot heighten people's awareness by documents, but by ecumenical experiences" that create "spaces of living in community and mutual support." "Based on the principles of the Reformation," said the president of the Latin American Council of Churches (CLAI), Israel Batista, "churches must concentrate their action on evangelization, ethics and spirituality."[19] So, God bless us!

19. World Council of Churches, *Minutes of the Fifty-Fifth Meeting: Porto Alegre, Brazil, 22–23 February 2006* (Geneva: WCC, 2006).

8

The Social and Economic Impact of John Calvin on the Korean Church and Society

Seong-Won Park

Korean Reformed and Presbyterian churches are built on the received doctrines brought over by American, Canadian, Australian, and Scottish missionaries. The Korean inheritance thus is not the original tradition initiated by the Reformers of the sixteenth century, but a form of Reformed Christianity whose original content had already been transformed and reduced by the time it arrived in Korea in the nineteenth century.

Before the missionaries came to Chosun, as the land was then called by the reigning dynasty of the time, lay Koreans who had been baptized by Scottish missionaries in Manchuria had started to spread the gospel back home. However, the Reformed tradition itself came into Korea at the hands of missionaries from Presbyterian churches in the United States, Canada, and Australia. Thus, its transmission from Geneva entailed a historic journey of three hundred years, spanning three continents and three different cultures. This long journey may have shaped Korean Reformed theology in a manner quite different from Calvin's understanding of the gospel and Christian witness.

Historically speaking, Reformed theology has been influenced by any number of movements, such as Puritanism, Separatism, Presbyterianism, Congregationalism, the Enlightenment, Pietism, the Great Awakenings, revivalism, and the missionary movement. Transmitting the Reformed understanding of the gospel from the United States to Korea added one more factor: the Korean context in which the Christian faith was introduced was entirely different socially, culturally, and religiously from those Western movements. The long-standing traditional religions in Korea were a significant feature of that context.

With this background, we can examine the kinds of political, social, and economic impacts the Reformed tradition—more precisely, Calvin's theological thought—has made in the Korean church and society. The most important theme across the board has been Calvin's emphasis on Christian witness.

THE BIBLE AND THE KOREAN CHURCH

The foremost characteristic of the Korean church might be its uncompromising loyalty to Scripture. The Bible has been placed at the center of Korean Christians' lives. Missionaries were eager to teach the Bible, and many Koreans became Christians by participating in Bible conferences. In the early Korean church, Sunday worship was celebrated at two o'clock in the afternoon; mornings were fully devoted to Bible study.

The Bible study tradition remains strong even today. Korean congregations hold numerous Bible courses and small Bible study groups. In some congregations, pastors train elders or deacons to become Bible study leaders. All Sunday school students take Bible courses according to the curriculum designed by the educational department of the general assembly of the churches. Every summer, Sunday schools conduct special conferences in which students participate in intensive Bible study courses.

Korean Christians regard the Bible as the most important resource for spiritual life. The key guiding principle comes from 2 Timothy 3:16–17: "All scripture is inspired by God and is useful for teaching, for reproof, for correction, and for training in righteousness, so that everyone who belongs to God may be proficient, equipped for every good work."

On the basis of this principle, most Korean Reformed Christians accept the literal inspiration of the Scriptures and regard the Bible as the fundamental text for Christian life and behavior.

In the Korean Presbyterian church, the Bible has supreme authority both in theology and in church policy. No matter how polemical they may be, theological arguments are accepted if their biblical reference is clear. No matter how understandable they may be, theological propositions are called into question, or at least rendered controversial, if their biblical reference is not clear. Sometimes the Korean church's biblical perspective can be too tough, too legalistic, and too literal. As far as the authority of the Bible is concerned, however, it still keeps its powerful hold in the Korean Presbyterian church.

The Bible has made a great contribution to Korean society. The Korean language, despised by Confucian intellectuals, was glorified by the Korean translation of the Bible. Many illiterate people learned to read and write through studying the Bible. Many women who had no opportunity to go to school encountered the joy of learning through the Bible. Liberation, emancipation, enlightenment, and spiritual nourishment are precious gifts granted by the Bible.

In this respect, Calvin's vision of the supreme authority of the Bible in Christian life and the Reformation principle of intelligibility have largely been achieved in the life of Korean Reformed Christians.

However, the authority of the Bible often became a source of division in the church as well. In fact, it can be said that the current divisions in the Korean church are largely rooted in different interpretations of Scripture.

The Korean church was deeply engaged in controversies around the question of biblical criticism in the 1930s. Those who believed without compromise in the literal and mechanical inspiration of the Bible were strongly opposed to those who were open to biblical criticism.

The leader of the first school was Park Hyeong Ryong. Having finished his basic studies in Soong Shil College and Keum Rung Theological Seminary in Nanjing, China, Park studied theology at Princeton Theological Seminary when it was under the theological leadership of J. Gresham Machen. He was deeply influenced as well by Charles Hodge and B. B. Warfield, who have become known as the "Orthodox" theologians to their Korean followers. Park finished his doctoral studies at the Southern Baptist Seminary in Louisville, Kentucky, where he was influenced by A. H. Strong. Along the way he also felt the impact of François Turretin, W. G. T. Shedd, Louis Berkhof, Abraham Kuyper, and L. B. Boettner. Park's theology is based on the literal inspiration of the Bible, predestination, salvation limited to the elect, and so forth.

Park was a kind of mentor for Korean Orthodox Reformed theology. All the Korean Presbyterian churches in the "Hapdong" denomination are in fact his faithful followers. A considerable number of theologians and pastors in the Presbyterian Church in Korea (PCK) regard Reformed theology in a similar way. Therefore, even today Park Hyeong Ryong's theological thought influences more than half of the Korean Presbyterian Christians.

This conservatism faced a series of challenges from progressive and liberal theologians and pastors in the 1930s, but every time they were challenged, the Orthodox group was successful in defeating liberalism and progressivism and casting their leading representatives out of the church. In 1934, the Rev. Kim Young Joo, who questioned Moses' authorship of the Pentateuch, was disciplined; in 1935, the Rev. Kim Choon Bae, who advocated women's rights, was disciplined; in 1935, the Rev. You Hyung Ki, who translated the Abingdon commentary, had to apologize for the "mistake" of translating a liberal commentary; and in 1947, Prof. Kim Jae Joon was expelled for advocating higher criticism in the sense of seeking to understand the social, historical, and cultural background in which biblical texts were written. His approach entailed as well historical and literary criticism, including analysis of form and style.

Among the progressive theologians, the Rev. Kim Jae Joon played a prominent role in introducing Christian social and political witness into Korean Christian theology. Having studied biblical criticism, Kim opposed notions of the literal inspiration of the Bible and promoted the importance of Christian witness for political and social justice. He is the founder of the Presbyterian Church in the Republic of Korea (PROK) and has played the role of mentor for the progressive theological line in the Korean Reformed community, particularly the political and social witness of the Korean Christians. *Minjung* theology was formed on the basis of his theological thought.

Another theological line stems from Chung Kyeong Ok, who had taught in the Methodist Theological Seminary in Seoul. He studied at Garrett Theological Seminary in Evanston, Illinois, where he was deeply influenced by Franklin Roll. His theological thought emerged under the influence of such leaders of the liberal school as Schleiermacher, Ritschl, Troeltsch, Herrmann, and Harnack. Not surprisingly, Chung introduced liberal religious theology into Korea, particularly emphasizing the importance of religious experience. He argued that truth can be revealed not only in the Christian gospel but also in other religious discourses. Along this line religious pluralism has been developed.

Even though in the Korean Reformed tradition other theological currents exist, such as the prosperity theology represented by the Pentecostal churches and the theology of personal conversion represented by the Baptist Church, one can say that the theological streams of the Reformed churches in Korea can be classified along these three different understandings of the Bible and the truth: the orthodox, the progressive, and the liberal.

CONFRONTATION BETWEEN CHRISTIAN HUMANISM AND CONFUCIAN FEUDALISM

Christianity was introduced to Korea when the country was in a critical period of social transition. Roman Catholicism was introduced into Korea in 1784, and Protestantism in 1884. The period from the end of the nineteenth century to the beginning of the twentieth is called the "Enlightenment period." At the end of the nineteenth century, a small-scale social reformation movement was initiated by a group of Reformed Confucians and some progressive intellectuals. They were eager to find a way by which they could carry out the reform of society, and in this searching process, they encountered Christianity in China.

They called Christianity *Seo Hak*, or "Western Science." Their reformation paradigm they called *Dong Do Seo Ki*, or "Eastern Ideology and Western Technology," thinking that by mixing the two different gifts of the East and the West they could reform society in a reasonable direction. The Korean reformers accepted not only Western technology but also the Western political system, and even its religion. Thus, the *Korean Christian Advocate*, the first Christian journal, declared on July 7, 1887:

> The Koreans say that Confucianism is the best. We don't want to degrade the teachings of Confucianism. However, it is evident that countries like England who don't know Confucianism and believe in God are well-civilized and strong, while China and Korea who are faithful to Confucianism are becoming weak. . . . Therefore we encourage you to enlighten yourselves by believing in God.

Christianity was warmly welcomed by those who were critical of the contemporary sociopolitical system, which featured the king as the ultimate center, a Confucian bureaucracy of aristocrats—the *Yangban* (nobility)—and a rigid social division between the *Yangban* and the Commoners (*Minjung*). Under such a highly stratified structure based on repressive Neo-Confucianism, peasants, slaves, and even middle-class people had been deprived of their basic human rights. They understood that the gospel had the potential to bring class equality to the social system in Korea, because there was no distinction between *Yangban* and Commoners in the gospel. The notion of the egalitarianism of the gospel strongly challenged the class system and contributed decisively to the elimination of formal class differences.

There is an impressive story related to this emancipation. There was "*Sangnom*," a kind of *dalit* class, in Korean society that included the butchers. The *Sangnom* were forbidden to marry outside of their caste, and in order to distinguish them from other people, they were not allowed to wear the hat of the gentry that every Korean man wore in those days. A butcher named Park who had become Christian made a request to the king through a missionary that the butchers be allowed to wear the hat of the *Yangban* gentry so that they also could enjoy their human dignity. Persuaded by the missionary, the king accepted this appeal. The butcher Park became one of the famous preachers who spread the liberating gospel to the repressive Korean society of that time; his son became the first Western medical doctor in Korea.

As to what kind of a contribution, positive or negative, Reformed theology has made with respect to the promotion of women's rights and dignity in Korea, the answer is unknown; close studies of Reformed theology in this connection would be worthwhile. In general, however, one can say in the first place that women, as the most oppressed people in Korean society, benefited from the liberating gospel. Christianity made a remarkable contribution to women's education and formal liberation, which had been forbidden in Confucian society. However, over the course of history, the rigid Reformed perspective on the Scriptures has always hindered the promotion of women's role in the church. Even today, the Hapdong denomination heavily criticize women's ordination in the Presbyterian Church of Korea (PCK) as a major mistake by the standards of Reformed orthodoxy.

CALVIN'S THEOCRACY AND THE SOCIOPOLITICAL WITNESS OF THE KOREAN CHURCH

The Christian faith also played a significant role in the political life of the Korean people during the process of social transition. The Korean Christian community had become influential in this regard already in 1895, when many Korean Christians participated in the *Dok Rip Hyop Hoe* (Independence Association), which launched the political reformation movement. Their ideal was the formation of a nation-state and the realization of an egalitarian society based on Western democracy. They were convinced that all nations, all people, and every member of society are equal before God, and that achieving equality among the people was an important goal of the social practice of the Christian faith.

In order to realize this vision, the Independence Association first advocated a republican polity, then a constitutional monarchy, as its political platform. Christians demanded that national policies should be decided by the will of the people. Since a republican polity was a revolutionary political idea under the monarch, Christian conviction meant the complete subversion of the Confucian monarchy and brought about a confrontation between the two.

An even stronger political witness arose in connection with the Korean church's protest against the Japanese occupation of the country, which was in process when Protestantism was introduced into Korea. The Korean Protestant community, therefore, began to see the Christian gospel as a possible spiritual resource for its independence movement.

After Japan defeated China and Russia in the Sino-Japanese (1894) and the Russo-Japanese (1904) wars, it managed to neutralize Great Britain with a treaty and entered the secret Taft-Katsura Agreement with the United States. The latter established mutual toleration of the colonization of Korea by Japan and of the Philippines by the United States. Korea fell into the hands of Japan and became its de facto colony; in 1905, a protectorate treaty was signed by force. In response, the Korean churches organized a number of prayer services for the national destiny.

Once colonial rule began to turn brutal after the treaty of 1905, the Christians' patriotic movement gradually switched from prayers to active anti-Japan struggles. Christians organized or joined various underground political organizations to struggle for national independence. One of them was the famous *Shin Min Hoe* (New People's Association). Its spirit was actually inherited from the Independence Association that had been dismantled by the king. Notably, in the Christians' participation in political activities they did not exclude the political dimension from the Christian witness, neither did they think that Christian faith had nothing to do with political purpose. *Shin Min Hoe* had several political programs, their basic idea being the creation of a new humanity that would have full sovereignty over its own existence.

The Japanese regarded the Korean Christian community as their most formidable force of resistance. In order to expel Christian influence from the independence movement and suppress that resistance, the Japanese fabricated the so-called Conspiracy Case to assassinate Governor General Terauchi. This was called the "105 Persons Incident," after the 105 leading persons who were prosecuted on fabricated charges. More than 80 percent of the people who were sentenced were Christian leaders. What the Korean Christians experienced through participation in the independence struggles was that to be spiritual was closely associated with being political, and that the political is deeply associated with being spiritual.

Korean Christians had the same experience through the famous March First Independence Movement (1919). Here too, the spiritual dimension of faith and the political dimension in witnessing to justice were intermingled with each other. This marked the peak of influence that the Korean Christian community had in both church and society. Together, the Christian community, the Dong Hak cultural nationalists, observers of indigenous religion, and Buddhists organized a national protest against the Japanese occupation. People continued demonstrations for three months, in some places for a year. The Christian community became a central part of the nonviolent and peaceful resistance movement, providing most of the rank and file and many of its leaders. Even though there were some discussions both of a theological and of a political nature about Christian participation in political activities, the general character of the Christian participation in the movement was unmistakable. At that time it was even said that to be a Christian meant to be involved in the movement.

Reformed theology became a particularly notable source for Korean Christians' participation in political witness. Of the 324 women who were arrested in the protests, 310 were Christian: specifically, 42 Methodists, one Catholic, 34 "other Protestants," and 233 Presbyterians.

Throughout those years of chaos, social upheaval, injustice, and national tragedy, many Koreans looked to the Christian church for comfort, protection, solidarity, and support. The Korean Christian community had strong credibility with the people, and the church did not betray the people's hope. In their own political context, Korean Christians read the book of Exodus and believed that the God who liberated the Israelites from Egyptian bondage would also liberate them from Japanese colonial rule. As the exodus was a historical event that became a decisive political paradigm in the formation of Israelite spirituality, it was from the struggle for independence against Japanese imperial power that the Christians of Korea came to know the biblical God who is at work in their historical situation. For Korean Christians, the independence movement was their exodus story, Japanese colonialism was their Egyptian bondage, and *Denno* (the Japanese emperor) was their Pharaoh. This is why Japanese authorities later banned the reading of the Old Testament from the pulpit.

Missionaries were not in favor of the Korean churches' political engagement. In fact, they endeavored to curb such anti-Japanese struggles for two reasons. First, they believed that the Christian faith had nothing to do with political activities and that the literal, pietistic faith they had cultivated in the church might be transmuted by such participation. Second, in a very political motive on their own part, they wished to be faithful to the demands of their own nations. The United States encouraged the missionaries to keep Korean Christians and churches from participating in the independence movement. One of the missionary's reports to the mission board of the Northern Presbyterian Church in the U.S.A. stated, "Missionaries had always mobilized all their efforts to prevent the Koreans from participating in politics."

Of course, a few missionaries supported the independence movement indirectly. But many missionaries were not supportive of the Koreans, and some actively supported Japan. When an article criticizing the missionaries appeared in the Japan *Times*, the Methodist bishop M. C. Harris wrote a rebuttal in the May 7, 1907, issue of the Yomiuri *Shinbun*, a Japanese paper:

> Our three leading missionaries (Johns, Scranton, and Harris) were threatened with death after we rejected the Koreans' request for assistance in their campaign to oppose the Japanese protectorate of Korea. . . . Please understand that missionaries are not the enemy of the Japanese people. Rather we, as the most faithful friends of Japan, work in concert to promote the well-being through Christian reconciliation between the Japanese and Korean people. . . . I would like to confess that I am the staunchest supporter of the [Japanese] resident-general's rule of Korea.

In spite of the consistent endeavors of the missionaries, Korean Christians defied and even betrayed the policy of the Korean mission, and continued to participate in the independence movement.

GOD'S SOVEREIGNTY AND THE *STATUS CONFESSIONIS* OF THE KOREAN CHURCH

In the 1930s, the assimilation policy of the Japanese colonial power began to turn very brutal. It aimed to eradicate Korean culture and history and to annihilate Korean identity. The Japanese forced Koreans to adopt Japanese names and to speak only Japanese in public places, including schools. Korean history disappeared from the curriculum. Finally, they forced the church to perform Shinto shrine worship, the Japanese national religion. Thus, the Korean churches faced the deepest crisis in their faith, because to worship in a Shinto shrine was to violate the First Commandment.

Thousands of Christians were jailed for refusing to bow at Shinto shrines. Many became martyrs. Some churches were forced to close down for their refusal. Although the Japanese said that Shinto worship was not a religious act but a national ceremonial ritual, for Christians it was a matter of being faithful to God or not. Just as Albert Camus said that history's amphitheater always contains martyrs and lions, the Korean church was in the amphitheater when faced with the challenge of Shinto shrine worship.

This spelled no less than a *status confessionis*. The Korean Christian community had to face the Japanese imperial power with its religious and absolute claims. Put otherwise, this was a sort of confrontation between the sovereignty of God and the Japanese emperor. The resistance or capitulation of the Korean Christian community was a question of resisting or giving in to the absolute authority of a political idol. Some argue that the martyrdom of the Christians in resistance to Shinto was a pure act of faith and therefore bore no political implications. But again we learn that faithfulness to the sovereignty of God cannot help but confront earthly power when it claims to be absolute.

However, most of the official churches capitulated and humiliated themselves at the Shinto shrine. This is one of the most shameful events in the history of Korean Christianity. The Korean Christian community, which had been so courageous until the 1920s, capitulated to the imperial power of Japan; then, without clear and creative discernment, it became naively anticommunistic at the liberation of the country in 1945 and during the Korean War in the beginning of the 1950s; next, it blindly supported the corrupt dictatorship led by Rhee Syng Man simply because he was a Christian. It is noteworthy that the 1940s was the time when the rate of church growth fell to its lowest ebb. The Korean churches' only notable activity in the 1950s was to divide.

MINJUNG THEOLOGY AS A KOREAN PARADIGM OF CALVIN'S SOCIAL AND ECONOMIC THOUGHT: A KOREAN REFORMED THEOLOGY

In the Korean context, the most vivid theological impact of Calvin's social and economic thought can be found in the *Minjung* theology and the *Minjung* church movement that emerged in the 1970s and 1980s in response to the economy-first policy driven by the dictator Park Chung Hee.

During the 1970s, Korean society experienced radical change when a military group seized power. Under the slogan of economic growth, Korean society was politically oppressed by the dictator and economically polarized between the haves and the have-nots. Society became unstable, and people were constantly worried about their security. Some committed Christians were deeply involved in the struggle for democracy, human rights, and freedom of conscience. In this social and political situation, the Korean church articulated *Minjung* theology. Many *Minjung* communities were established in industrial areas where the poor, the oppressed, and workers were living, suffering, and struggling. *Minjung* denotes the people who are politically oppressed, socially alienated, economically deprived, and religiously marginalized, although they play a major role in making history.

Minjung theology was not articulated in a theological academy. It started where people were suffering and oppressed. In 1957, a small group of committed urban industrial missionaries began their work to evangelize the laborers. From 1968 on, some of them extended their efforts to the urban poor and poor farmers. Their approach at the beginning was very traditional—teaching doctrine and converting and baptizing workers. However, the problem with this approach was that it did not work very well. The workers' language, concerns, perceptions, and life situations were so alien that the evangelists could not communicate with them.

The evangelists had to find a new way to communicate with the *Minjung*. The way they discovered was to live and work among the workers, farmers, and urban poor. Industrial mission evangelists became factory workers and labored alongside the real workers. They experienced the same frustrations, despair, fear, anger, and weariness as the workers experienced. Through these extraordinary experiences, they discovered a new way of communicating. This communication was not "from us to the workers," but in the opposite direction, "from the workers to the mission evangelists." The evangelists realized that the "prepackaged gospel" could not be communicated to the workers or the poor. Everyone began to reread the Bible, together with the workers, from the workers' perspective. This was the beginning of a most remarkable process of rediscovering the power of the gospel and the Bible as a liberating message, relevant to the life of *Minjung*.

The industrial evangelists began to ask theological questions of the biblical texts on the basis of workers' perception and the perspective they themselves had newly learned from the *Minjung*. On the basis of these questions, a small group of theologians began to articulate a *Minjung* theology. That opened a new theological horizon. Some theologians, such as Suh Nam Dong, tried to articulate systematic theology from the *Minjung* perspective, while others tried to explore the *Minjung* theme in the Bible. Church history was reassessed from the point of view of cultural analysis by historians and theologians such as Hyun Yong Hak and Suh Kwang Sun.

Minjung theology led to the development of a new way of doing theology. It began to discover the God who is at work in the *Minjung* movement. For *Minjung* theology, Christology refers not simply to an individual event related to a person called Jesus. Rather, Christ is present in the *Minjung* event whose struggle for justice and liberation is accompanied by the liberating God, as was the case in the exodus. God's engagement in history is demonstrated or revealed in the liberation event.

On this theological assumption, *Minjung* theology discovered the Christ event in the cross-bearing, struggling, and suffering of Chun Bong Joon, who initiated a peasant movement in protest against oppressive feudal society. Another manifestation of the Christ event took place in the act of self-immolation by Chun Tae Il in protest against the terrible working conditions faced by the young laborers in the Pyeong Hwa (Peace) Market. He was a sincere Christian and gave his life for the human rights of the workers who were endlessly being exploited. This event awakened students to an awareness of workers' human rights and challenged them to commit themselves to defending those rights and the dignity of the workers. This also provoked the principle that theology was no longer a work of intellectual speculation but a concrete response to Christ events that occurred in the midst of *Minjung* in their struggle for the advent of the kingdom of God.

Minjung theology raised a new question about the presence of Christ. In response to the Roman Catholic Church, which argues that Christ is present in the bread and wine during the mass, the Reformed community argues that Christ is present in the proclamation of the gospel. *Minjung* theology has a different understanding from both: Christ is present in the midst of the *Minjung*'s struggle and suffering for God's justice and God's peace. The majority of mainline Reformed churches in Korea give the Eucharist a strong soteriological meaning. In the *Minjung* theological understanding, however, the Eucharist expresses the value of the kingdom of God on earth and affirms the covenant of divine solidarity that God initiates with the *Minjung*. The liturgical celebration of Communion is a messianic banquet understood eschatologically. Understood in a more dynamic context, it is a type of solidarity meal in a situation where all members risk being arrested after celebrating it together. The Lord's Table that *Minjung* community members celebrated is this kind of solidarity meal—not just an ordinary solidarity meal but a divine one, a full sharing in the significance of the cross, since the participants might face arrest afterward.

Minjung theology has been called a Korean liberation theology. But it has gone beyond Latin American Liberation Theology by becoming a struggle to liberate Korean theology from its narrow dualistic spirituality. In this sense, *Minjung* theology is an attempt to renew Christian spirituality. It is a theology of renewal of faith and witness, opening itself to the political and social realm to make the faith relevant to the historical reality in which people are living. The Reformation attempted in sixteenth-century Europe to reform the mystified spirituality of the medieval, hierarchical church. In this sense, *Minjung* theology might be a Korean Reformed theology.

CONCLUDING REMARK

A Swiss friend of mine told me that one needs to distinguish between "Calvinist" and "Calvinian." "Calvinist" refers to the Reformed churches and those who have followed the teaching of those churches throughout time and in different places. "Calvinian" refers to Calvin's own teaching and its spirit. The rediscovery of Calvin's own teaching in the twentieth century has revived Calvinian values, even if its defenders sometimes criticize Calvin himself. There are two different types of followers of Calvin in Korea. Unfortunately, the majority of Korean Presbyterians are Calvinist. Just as Max Weber mistakenly portrayed Calvin's economic thought by concentrating his research on the economic thought of the Puritans in the seventeenth and eighteenth centuries, Korean Calvinists introduced into Korea seventeenth-century Calvinists'—particularly Dutch Calvinists'—orthodox theology as Calvin's authentic theology. For that we are paying a high price with respect to church divisions and the rigidity of Christian existence in society.

However, there are also no small numbers of Calvinians who are articulating Korean Reformed theology in line with Calvin's spirit of the authentic witness that is required in a particular context. It is my hope that someday Korean Reformed theology itself can enrich Calvin's vision of that witness.

9

Calvin, Calvinism, and Capitalism

The Challenges of New Interest in Asia

Christoph Stückelberger

My recent experiences in China and Indonesia have provoked the question: Why is there a new interest in Max Weber's analysis *The Protestant Ethic and the Spirit of Capitalism* in Southeast Asia today? Three years ago, a delegation of Chinese governmental representatives for religious affairs (officially still Marxists) visited Switzerland to study the role of religion for society. I explained to them in a speech the relevance of Christian economic ethics based on Calvin, which was new to them. They showed a profound interest in my point that Calvin did not invent exploitative capitalism but defended the interests of the weak and the poor in his concept of a socially responsible economy.

Last year on my way back from China as visiting lecturer I saw Max Weber's book *The Protestant Ethic and the Spirit of Capitalism* in English and Chinese in a prominent place in the airport bookshop. I found the same in the Indonesian language in the airport bookshop in Jakarta this year on my way to Duta Wacana Christian University in Yogyakarta, where I was asked to give lectures on "The Role of Christianity and Islam on the Development of Capitalism, with a Special View on Calvin the Reformer." In this essay I will try to sharpen the question and contribute a few elements of a possible answer.

IS THERE REALLY A NEW INTEREST IN CALVINISM AND CAPITALISM?

Let's test this question with the support of the Google search engine (which only gives some indications). I counted the number of references for the combination of keywords in seven countries, such as "Max Weber (and) John Calvin (in) China."

Key: A Google search of "John Calvin" combined with "China" yielded 616,000 references; "John Calvin" and "Indonesia" yielded 97,600. The figures on the top line show the results of a search in December 2004; those on the lower line, the results from August 29, 2005. The significant difference might reflect the addition of new data systems and more differentiated search methods.

	China	*Indonesia*	*South Korea*	*India*	*South Africa*	*Chile*	*Kenya*
John Calvin	120,000*	18,100	30,700	86,000	80,400	20,200	17,000
	616,000	*97,600*	*536,000*	*391,000*	*667,000*	*73,400*	*63,600*
Max Weber	137,000	53,900	57,900	105,000	76,600	90,300	11,300
	790,000	*162,000*	*168,000*	*483,000*	*255,000*	*335,000*	*42,000*
Max Weber John Calvin	4,240	1,690	1,490	3,110	3,860	736	922
	55,800	*9,930*	*12,500*	*26,700*	*23,800*	*15,000*	*6,800*
John Calvin Capitalism	7,950	3,330	4,090	6,670	6,920	3,280	2,880
	184,000	*8,930*	*17,000*	*125,000*	*35,100*	*11,000*	*5,320*
John Calvin Capitalism 21 century	2,990	647	817	2,510	2,800	609	398
	24,300	*7,220*	*11,900*	*16,700*	*22,900*	*6,570*	*3,800*
John Calvin Predestination	971	448	534	1,870	975	115	265
	7,520	*805*	*653*	*8,010*	*8,240*	*525*	*489*
Calvin Klein*	*588,000*	*46,200*	*272,000*	*168,000*	*448,000*	*71,700*	*25,000*

*This figure would be much less if we excluded, e.g., the company "John Calvin Jones China."
**Famous global textile brand of the Dutch company.

I have chosen emerging markets in South and Southeast Asia and, for the sake of comparison, emerging markets in Africa and Latin America. The table shows a relatively great interest in Calvin the Reformer, but more in Max Weber, in the main countries in Southeast and South Asia. The interest also exists in growing or transition economies such as South Africa's, much less in other developing countries such as Kenya. The figures obviously show the greater interest in Calvin's economic message than in his theological foundations (see "Calvin predestination"). Of course, Google statistics are limited in their value because they reflect only people working with the Internet (in English) in a country and publications mentioned on the Internet. Many publications that are not on the Internet are not represented in these figures. Nevertheless, they show tendencies of the debate at least in Anglophone countries and where English is a common language in academic and business circles.

New publications are another indicator of the growing interest in Max Weber's views on Calvinism. Since the late seventies and early eighties, a growing number of translations of Max Weber and John Calvin have been published in Southeast Asia, especially in China. Not only the Chinese edition of Weber's *Protestant Ethic and the Spirit of Capitalism*, but also his famous book *The Religion of China: Confucianism and Taoism* plays a role. Secondary publications analyze the role of Protestantism and Confucianism in today's China.[1] Calvin himself and his books are much less known and translated, but I do not yet have a good overview of it. Rachel Xiaohong Zhu, lecturer in the Religious Studies Program, Department of Philosophy of Fudan University in Shanghai, told me, "Most of Weber's writings have been translated into Chinese. There are a lot of research papers on Weber too. But Calvin's theology is not a popular topic for scholars in universities or other academic institutes."

Some first conclusions:

There is a growing interest in capitalism and Calvinism especially in Southeast Asia, as shown in statistics and publications.

There is a growing interest in the relation between economy, religion, and culture.

WHY THIS GROWING INTEREST?

I see three main reasons for this growing interest:

The Political and Economic Orientation

The geopolitical changes in 1989—with the collapse of Soviet Communism, with globalization and its integration of almost all economies into the neoliberal type of market economy, and with the fast economic growth of the "Tigers" in Southeast Asia—made it necessary to redefine capitalism and to reorient former attitudes toward capitalism. In China, a kind of reconciliation

1. See, e.g., Tu Wei-ming, "Confucian Ethics and the Entrepreneurial Spirit in East Asia," in *Confucian Ethics Today: The Singapore Challenge* (Singapore: Federal Publications, 1984); Karin Fiedler, *Wirtschaftsethik in China am Fallbeispiel von Shanghaier Protestanten zwischen Marx und Mammon* (Hamburg: Institut für Asienkunde, 2000).

between Chinese socialism and Western capitalism became reality; in India, the shift from economic protectionism to economic liberalization led to ideological confrontations.

Aiming Wang, dean of the famous Nanjing (China) Union Theological Seminary, answered my question about why Weber arouses more interest in China today:

> The Chinese scholars in the late 1980s at Beijing University started a very serious debate about the Weberian judgment of capitalism and Calvin by articles and publications. The reputation of the rational and modern capitalism with the inner spirit of the Protestantism has been formed by the publications of Weber in China since 1986, which is opposed to the orthodox definition of capitalism by the ideas of Marxism-Leninism in China during nearly one century. Calvin had a very bad image in China. The Three-Self-Movement of Chinese churches did not allow emphasizing the foreign roots of theology. Calvin was seen as opposite to Chinese socialism. The studies of Weber introduced the signification of John Calvin to Chinese intellectuals' minds, especially those open to modernization of the Chinese economy.

Max Weber was trying to explain the rise of capitalism by identifying the Protestant ethic as the variable that had an "elective affinity" with the emergence of capitalism. In his book on capitalism and human rights in China, Michael Santoro uses Weber's methodology to describe how modern multinational corporations have an "elective affinity" to human rights and "do have a positive human rights spin-off effect," because they contribute to economic prosperity, which strengthens democracy and human rights.[2] This position is questionable, because it defends the wrong trickle-down theory, saying that economic growth per se contributes to more prosperity for all and better respect of human rights. Empirical studies show that the reality is much more complex: multinational companies strengthen some human rights in some situations and weaken or violate them in others.

Values: Calvinism, Confucianism, Islam, Asian Values

The interest in Max Weber and Calvinism is linked not only to the shift from socialism to capitalism in many countries but also to the broad debate on religious values and their influence on the economy. In China, the revival of Confucianism (as well as Buddhism), in Indonesia the conflict between Muslim and Christian communities, and in India the political power of Hindu fundamen-

2. Michael A. Santoro, *Profits and Principles: Global Capitalism and Human Rights in China* (Ithaca, NY: Cornell University Press, 2000), 42–43.

talists has brought the debate on the religious foundations of economic development back to the fore.

Max Weber emphasized eighty years ago the relationship between "Confucian rationalism" and the "rationalism of Protestantism" and saw parallel virtues and values in Confucianism and Puritanism that today are now again discussed in China.[3] The Swiss Catholic theologian Hans Küng wrote in his book *Christianity and the Chinese Religion* in the late eighties: "Even Western business people now recognize that it was the Confucian spirit which stood behind East Asian economic growth." Küng adds, "The wish to strengthen Confucian values does not mean that one expects faster modernization from it, but rather that one hopes it will serve as a corrective to patent accompanying features of modernization like extreme individualism or moral permissiveness."[4] The debate on Weber and Calvinism in China can therefore not be separated from the debate on the contribution of Confucianism to the modern economy and its ethical correction by moral limits and norms.

In order to avoid dependency on Western values, the debate on Asian values became important in the mid-nineties.[5] It included directly and indirectly a critique of Western values, holding that economic success is not only, and not primarily, based on Western (Calvinist) values but on homemade Asian ones. But with the financial crash and crisis in Southeast Asia in the late nineties, the defenders of Asian values became more quiet and defensive because the question came up of why these values could not avoid the painful crash.

During that crisis, it was easier to look for another scapegoat. That might be one of the reasons for the debate on Max Weber and Calvinism in Indonesia. Muslims tried to blame Christians, especially Chinese Christians in Indonesia, for the crisis. This shows the ambiguity: on one hand, Max Weber's view of Calvinism and its work ethic seemed to explain the success of the modern Western economy; this provoked the jealousy of non-Christian and non-Western communities. On the other hand, Protestantism/Calvinism was held responsible not only for the success but also for the failures and new poverty in Indonesia. My suspicion, after various dialogues with Indonesian scholars, is that the root of the debate on Max Weber and Calvinism in Indonesia is a debate among Christian confessions (Protestants and Catholics) as well as between Christian and Muslim economic ethics. The fact that Muslim scholars in Indonesia publish more and more studies on Muslim business ethics and

3. Max Weber, *Die Wirtschaftsethik der Weltreligionen: Konfuzianismus und Taoismus: Schriften 1915–1920* (Tübingen: J. C. B. Mohr, 1991), 193–208.

4. Hans Küng and Julia Ching, *Christentum und Chinesische Religion* (Munich: Piper, 1988), 113. My translation.

5. See William Theodore de Bary, *Asian Values and Human Rights: A Confucian Communitarian Perspective* (Cambridge, MA: Harvard University Press, 1998).

other themes of economic ethics such as work ethics confirms the growing interest in the religious foundations of economic values.

Looking for Cultural Factors of Economic Growth

I asked my colleague Yahya Wijaya, professor of ethics at the Duta Wacana Christian University in Yogyakarta (who wrote his doctoral thesis on business ethics in Indonesia[6]), about the reasons for the growing interest in Weber in Indonesia. He answered, "I think there is a growing awareness of the role of culture in shaping the economy. Here in Indonesia, talks on 'work ethic' seem to be more common. It may be related to attempts to recover the Indonesian economy after the crisis, attempts which seem to face so many obstacles. Many firms are relocating to other countries, partly for security reasons, partly for economic ones. They go where they find more productive societies probably due to a higher work ethic. The issue is also discussed in relation to the rise of China as a new superpower. Weber is often referred to, quite often critically."

That summarizes the reasons for the growing interest in Weber and Calvinism in transition economies in Southeast and South Asia. Economic development cannot be understood and explained purely by economic and political analysis. Religious and cultural factors have to be included and respected.

CALVIN STOOD FOR A SOCIALLY RESPONSIBLE ECONOMY AND AGAINST EXPLOITATION

In *The Protestant Ethic and the Spirit of Capitalism*, Weber was interested in finding proofs for his sociological methodology of the history of ideas, but he only cites Calvin himself once in over a hundred pages of footnotes! My guess is that Weber did not read Calvin but only secondary literature about him, perhaps because he could not read French. On the other hand, he quotes Luther several times from his original works in German. Weber admits in a footnote, "I may here say definitely that we are not studying the personal views of Calvin, but Calvinism, and that in the form to which it had evolved by the end of the sixteenth and in the seventeenth centuries in the great areas where it had a decisive influence and which were at the same time the home of capitalistic culture."[7]

Today there is enough historical evidence that capitalism in its modern industrial form did not yet exist during Calvin's time and cannot directly be

6. Yahya Wijaya, *Business, Family, and Religion: Public Theology in the Context of the Chinese-Indonesian Business Community* (Oxford: Peter Lang, 2002).

7. Max Weber, *The Protestant Ethic and the Spirit of Capitalism*, trans. Talcott Parsons (1930; repr., London: Routledge, 1996), 220n7.

deduced from his teaching.[8] The famous Swiss theologian and church historian Max Geiger puts this conclusion simply: "A relationship between Calvin (Calvinism) and capitalism cannot be seen."[9] The historical development from the Middle Ages to modernity, including economic development, is much more complicated than a direct link between Calvin and capitalism suggests.

Many people believe that Max Weber describes Calvin's thoughts. In fact, he only describes a specific form of Puritanism (the one of seventeenth-century English noncomformist Richard Baxter), which is in many aspects very different from or even opposite to Calvin's teaching. Weber himself made this clear in the footnote quoted above, wherein he continues: "For the present, Germany is neglected entirely because pure Calvinism never dominated large areas here. Reformed is, of course, by no means identical with calvinistic."[10]

The differences between Calvin and Puritanism are obvious: Puritanism wanted to work hard for the glory of God, but Calvin's work ethic emphasized that work helps to free us from dependency on others, to live in dignity, and to help the needy. Similar differences can be shown related to the use of time, the understanding of wealth and luxury, the division of labor, the attitude toward sexuality, asceticism, the accumulation of wealth, and predestination.

In addition, we need a clearer analysis of the different forms of capitalism. Commercial capitalism, industrial capitalism, and today's information capitalism are different. The forms of market economy at the time of Calvin and of Puritanism are different from industrial capitalism at the time of Max Weber and today. Calvin has to be translated into our time and economic context. An excellent example is *Calvin's Economic and Social Thought*, written by the Swiss economist and Reformed theologian André Biéler in 1961 and only recently published in English.[11]

The World Alliance of Reformed Churches (WARC), in part together with the Lutheran World Federation (LWF) and the World Council of Churches (WCC), has detected the critical potential of Protestant theology based on the Reformers and especially Calvin in the modern neoliberal economy. At the end of a controversial *processus confessionis*, WARC at its twenty-fourth General Assembly in Accra, Ghana, in 2004 adopted the text "Covenanting for Justice in the Economy and the Earth," also called the "Accra Confession."[12] Based

8. Max Geiger, "Calvin, Calvinismus, Kapitalismus," in *Gottesreich und Menschenreich: Ernst Staehelin zum 80. Geburtstag*, ed. Max Geiger (Basel: Helbing and Lichtenhahn, 1969), 262.

9. Ibid., 286.

10. Weber, *Protestant Ethic*, 220n7.

11. André Biéler, *Calvin's Economic and Social Thought* (Geneva: WARC/WCC, 2005).

12. *Accra 2004, Protocol of the 24th General Assembly of the World Alliance of Reformed Churches* (Geneva: WARC, 2005), appendix 13.

on Reformed ethics, it clearly states its resistance against all forms of exploitative economy that accumulate power and capital in the hands of a few and that—in its neoliberal form—justifies extremist freedom that is not linked to justice and sustainability. The Federation of Swiss Reformed Churches has transmitted the WARC efforts to Swiss reality with its position paper "Globalance," which calls, in response to WARC, for a globalization with a human face—"globalance" as a balance of values such as freedom and justice.[13]

AN EXAMPLE: CALVIN'S ETHICS OF INTEREST

An example of Calvin's challenging economic ethics remains his profound view of fair interest rates. Up to the time of the Reformation it was forbidden to charge interest in Europe, not least due to the prohibition of taking interest in the Old Testament (Exod. 22:25; Deut. 23:19–20). However, this prohibition was actually eroded by many exceptions. Calvin took a fundamentally positive attitude to the charging of interest. He justified his attitude by maintaining that the intention of the biblical prohibition was to protect one's neighbor and especially the poor and weak. Hence, service to one's neighbor was vital also in matters of charging interest. He was led by the eighth commandment, "Do not steal" (Exod. 20:15), and by the Golden Rule, "In everything do to others as you would have them do to you" (Matt. 7:12). He developed "seven restrictions" as guidelines to charging interest.

The first restriction is that "the poor should not be charged interest nor should anyone be under constraint who is afflicted by disaster or is in a situation of utter need through their poverty. . . . The second restriction is that those who lend should not be so set on gain that they are in default in necessary charitable works, nor so concerned to put their money in safe keeping that they fail to recognize the value of their poor brothers and sisters. . . . The third restriction is that [in the case of an interest-bearing loan] nothing should happen that does not accord with natural justice, and should not be found to be appropriate everywhere when we look at the matter in accordance with Christ's injunction (i.e. what you want others to do for you etc.). . . . [The fourth restriction is that] the borrower should make as much or more profit from the borrowed money [as the creditor]. . . . Fifthly, let us not consider what is allowable in terms of received common custom, nor assess what is right and fair by the iniq-

13. Federation of Swiss Protestant Churches, "Globalance: Christian Perspectives on Globalisation with a Human Face." Summary in English and full text in German and French at http://www.sek-feps.ch.

uitous standards of the world, but let us use the Word of God as a precept. . . . Sixthly, let us not consider only what is of advantage to the individual with whom we have to deal, but consider also what is expedient for the public, for quite clearly the interest paid by a trader is a public allowance. Thus, one must properly determine that the contract is of service generally, rather than harmful. . . . Seventhly, let us not break the standard that the civil laws of the region or locality allow—though that is not always enough, because these laws permit things that they would not be able to correct or suppress by forbidding them. So we have to prefer fairness, which cuts back on excesses."[14]

SPREADING THE INFLUENCE OF CALVIN'S ECONOMIC ETHICS

To Participate Actively in the Debate in Order to Correct Instrumentalization

This positive chance to include religious factors in economic development is at the same time a great challenge. The use and abuse of Calvin through the eyes of a popular reading of Max Weber shows the danger of instrumentalizing religion in order to accuse or excuse certain developments. Scientific honesty requires that theologians and those who know Calvin's teaching be more present in these debates among economists, politicians, and sociologists. In many countries there are not enough well-trained theologians who can raise an expert voice.

To Read Calvin and Not Only Max Weber on Calvinism

Yahya Wijaya from Yogyakarta confesses, "There is little attention to Calvin, even among Indonesian 'Calvinists.'" We can overcome unfair instrumentalization only by going back to the roots and sources. Calvin himself must be read instead of reading "only" Max Weber. Theological students have to be invited to study Calvin, especially his careful theological justification of his ethical vision and values. Scholars of economics, sociology, politics, and comparative religions should be invited to study Calvin in order to correct their

14. The quoted text is drawn from Biéler, *Calvin's Economic and Social Thought*, 406–7; Biéler's French-based "exception" I have rendered as "restriction" as more in keeping with Calvin's original. See also Christoph Stückelberger, *Global Trade Ethics* (Geneva: WCC, 2002), 161; Edward Dommen, "Calvin et le prêt à intérêt," *Finance et Bien Commun/Finance and Common Good* 16 (2003): 42–58.

prejudices and wrong perceptions. Textbooks have to be revised, and politicians have to be involved in dialogue where they instrumentalize Calvin for their different purposes. That is not only a question of historical truth and intellectual honesty. It is a vital question for the public perception of Protestant churches in the world, especially in the economic and political sector in emerging markets and transition countries.

To Support Good Scientific Translations

Aiming Wang from Nanjing wrote to me: "The Chinese edition of Max Weber's book on Calvinism and capitalism was translated from Parsons's version in English. That is not a very serious version. I've compared it with the French version and through my professor in Neuchâtel with the original German version of Weber himself, which shows serious differences." This shows the importance of good scientific translations not only of Max Weber but also of Calvin. I therefore highly appreciate the scientific translation of André Biéler into English. I do not have an overview of Calvin's books in Chinese, Indonesian, Korean, Tamil, Thai, or Swahili, but their quality is worth examining.

To Resist Monocausal Explanations

Instrumentalization happens in order to achieve a specific political or economic goal. For this goal, the complexity of reality is often reduced to monocausal explanations. Scientific honesty requires one to resist these temptations and to analyze the multicausal roots of economic developments. That leads to acknowledging the influence, but also the limits of the influence, of Calvin on economic developments. Only if one analyzes each country, and even the different regions, sectors, and classes in a country, can one see the complexity of factors.[15]

The Calvin Jubilee in 2009: An Opportunity to Correct Wrong Perceptions of Calvin

Calvin's 500th birthday will be celebrated in 2009. Churches around the world, including the churches in Geneva and the Federation of Swiss Protestant Churches, are already preparing for this event. In the light of today's urgent challenges in economic, business, social, and political ethics, it is important to bring to light Calvin's helpful ethical approaches, which show the way to an economy with a human face and a development ethics that reduces the gap

15. This challenge is well expressed in Fareed Zakaria, "Asian Values—Engine of Economic Growth?" *Daily Times* (Pakistan), November 2, 2004, 1.

between poor and rich. Calvin is a forerunner of a socially (and environmentally, we add today) responsible economy; his clear and discriminating ethic of taking interest is a good example. This economy respects free decision as a result of Christian faith but is at the same time inseparably linked to mechanisms of corporate social responsibility and empathy for the weak. This leads to mechanisms of redistribution of wealth and strong responsibilities of the state with its laws and the church with its diaconal and prophetic role.

PART 3

Challenges in Translating John Calvin

Texts and Contexts

10

Translating Calvin into English

EDWARD DOMMEN

John Calvin has a disagreeable reputation in the English-speaking world. This is easier to understand when one compares the English translations of his works to the originals. The numerous nineteenth- and twentieth-century translations, which are the ones most readily available today, systematically bias his arguments.

Calvin was quickly translated into English in his lifetime. Indeed, he was a best-seller. In the mid-seventeenth century, a time when religious ideas were vigorously debated in England to the point of civil war, Richard Baxter was one of the most prolific Puritan writers and best-known preachers in the country. Yet Calvin sold better in England than Baxter. From what little I have seen, the early translations are faithful to the original, but they have a drawback of their own: their language is outdated. It recalls the style of the King James Bible, and that introduces another form of distraction for present-day users. For that reason, as well as the fact that they are harder to come by, they are less used today.

The intentions behind the translations of Calvin help to explain some of the misunderstandings of his teaching not only in the English-speaking world but in areas where English serves as an international working language.

In translating André Biéler's *Calvin's Economic and Social Thought*, James Greig made the decision not to retranslate the quotations from Calvin but to use existing ones. The choice can easily be defended: the passages are more likely to be known to scholars working in English, and they can more readily be relocated back in their textual context. But as I was revising Greig's work,

I came to realize that the distortions in the translations had systematic features. The purpose of this essay is to describe them by means of illustrations drawn from the passages quoted in Biéler. They generally called for correction. As a result, most of them are described in the notes indicating their source as "based on so-and-so's translation." The examples presented here are drawn from a short sequence of pages, but similar ones can be found throughout the book. It suffices to present here a single example of each type of bias.

THE TROUBLE WITH MONUMENTS

By the nineteenth century, Calvin had had ample time to become a monument. Monuments are larger than life and free from the contingencies of getting on with the business of everyday living. Calvin himself, however, was a man of the spoken word. Much of his teaching was oral, addressed to an audience that was in front of him. He used everyday popular language. This helped keep the audience attentive during his long sermons. "Those who think that the Pharisees laughed at Christ for being content with common and simple language and not making a bombastic display by affecting exquisite terms which fill the mouth nicely have not weighed Saint Luke's words sufficiently."[1] (In other words, what really worried the Pharisees was the substance of the message, which was attractively dressed in common and simple language.)

Calvin's language was picturesque, lively, and often earthy. The nineteenth-century translators found that difficult to reconcile with his status as a monument.

Example 1

Les Prophètes . . . ne veulent pas cependant occuper l'esprit des fidèles pour s'amuser à l'auge comme des pourceaux . . . , comme si notre Seigneur voulait seulement farcir la panse des siens et les engraisser en ce monde. (AB, 309)[2]

The Prophets . . . intend not to fill the minds of the godly with thoughts about eating and drinking . . . as though the Lord intended to gratify their appetites. (John Owen 1846)

The Prophets . . . intend not to fill the minds of the faithful with the joys of the trough like piglets . . . as though our Lord intended simply to stuff the bellies of his own and fatten them up in this world. (ABE, 272)

1. ABE, 279. References prefixed "ABE" are to page numbers in André Biéler, *Calvin's Economic and Social Thought* (Geneva: WARC/WCC, 2005), where the full reference to Calvin's original text will in turn be found.

2. In all the examples in this essay, the text in italics is the original French as presented in Biéler, the ordinary text is the version of the translator named, and that in bold is the corrected version of it. References prefixed "AB" are to page numbers in Biéler, *La pensée économique et sociale de Calvin* (Geneva: Georg, 1961).

Gratifying the appetites of the godly conveys a more genteel picture than stuffing the bellies of piglets! But the change has deeper significance.

GOD GAVE US LIFE IN THIS WORLD TO ENJOY IN ABUNDANCE

Note the disappearance of the key word "simply" in Owen's translation. God does indeed intend to satisfy the material needs of the faithful, but he intends more than just that. As Biéler sums it up, "While God does indeed promise his people the rich blessings of the earth, this is not so that he can put all the emphasis simply on these signs, but rather so that they can attain to the spiritual realities" (ABE, 272). Calvin did not teach the dour asceticism of the Puritans. As Biéler said elsewhere, the Reformed vision is "not a severe asceticism, but joyous sobriety and lucid generosity."[3]

This bowdlerization is not just nineteenth-century prudery. It fits into the desire to spiritualize, to render otherworldly, what Calvin intended to refer to the here and now.

Example 2
méchant (AB, 293, 304)
ungodly (T. H. L. Parker 1959; Beveridge 1845)
wicked (ABE, 257, 267)

Such spiritualization turns people away from striving to mend the world. William Penn, a Quaker strongly influenced by the Reformation (he studied at the Protestant academy at Saumur under Moyse Amyraut), reflected Calvin's position in the pithy phrase, "True godliness don't turn [people] out of the world but enables them to live better in it and excites their endeavours to mend it."

Such turning away is strikingly reflected in example 3. There is indeed a world of difference between rendering worship free and upholding the service of God in the realm of politics in general and justice in particular. Indeed, the very next sentence in Calvin's text continues explicitly, "But still there are thoughtless people who make them [i.e., kings] too spiritual."

Example 3
Voici donc ce qui est principalement requis des rois, qu'ils usent du glaive que Dieu leur a mis en main pour maintenir son service en sa pureté. (AB, 294)
. . . to render free the worship of God (John Owen 1846)
. . . **to uphold his service in its purity** (ABE, 258)

3. Biéler, *Réhabiliter l'argent* (Lausanne: Action de Carême/Pain pour le prochain, 1984), 32. Cf. footnote 6 on p. 55 of this volume.

In example 4 we find both the dourness and the otherworldliness combined. As for dourness, "desire for *it*" introduces a reference back to a more liberal use of possessions, making that, rather than greed, reprehensible. As for otherworldliness, Calvin is referring here not to sin but to a social relationship.

Example 4

Non pas qu'user des créatures un peu au large soit une chose damnable en soi, mais la convoitise *est toujours* vicieuse. (AB, 313)

Not that a more liberal use of possessions should be condemned as bad in itself, but a desire for *it* is always *sinful.* (Smail 1964, based perhaps on Pringle [1848–49, 1851])

. . . but *greed* is always *perverse* (ABE, 275)

Calvin systematically refers to Jesus Christ as "Jesus the man" and "Christ the anointed." The translators (e.g., Parker [1972] and Beveridge) often omit the Jesus, thus focusing on the Christ, as in example 5. Example 5 also illustrates another way of spiritualizing Calvin's concern with the here and now: something permanent endures through time, while the eternal is generally seen as timeless. The word "eternal" appears frequently in the King James Version (KJV) of the Bible, normally conjoined with "life" or occasionally "damnation." The contrast is clear in 2 Corinthians 5:1: "We have a building of God, a house not made with hands, eternal in the heavens." The house built with hands may nonetheless be permanent. The word "permanent" does not appear in the KJV. It appears just once in the Segond translation of the Bible into French, in 2 Corinthians 3:11, where it corresponds to the English phrase "that which remains." If Calvin, who knew the Bible like the back of his hand, chose the unbiblical term "permanent," it was surely no accident.

Example 5

Jésus-Christ a une puissance permanente. (AB, 303)

Christ is armed with *eternal* power. (Beveridge 1845)

Jesus Christ is armed with *permanent* power. (ABE, 266)

ME AND EVERYONE ELSE

Calvin often hails his listeners, addressing them directly. It is part of his oral style. The translators frequently turn his call into impersonal statements so that they no longer aim at anyone in particular (the shift from "our Lord" to "the Lord" in example 1 is another instance in the same vein).

Example 6

. . . *nous commande* (AB, 308)

. . . bids the fearers of God (Anderson 1845)

. . . bids us (ABE, 271)

Replacing Calvin's present tense by the past tense has a similar effect. In example 7 a statement about a perpetual feature of social reality becomes a description of somewhere long ago and far away.

Example 7

. . . *tant les étrangers que les orphelins et veuves sont presque destitués de tout secours et aide* (AB, 299)

. . . strangers as well as orphans and widows *were* almost destitute of protection and assistance (John Owen 1846)

. . . strangers as well as orphans and widows *are* almost destitute of protection and assistance (ABE, 262)

The end result of these turns of translation is to insulate readers. They no longer feel that they are being directly addressed and called to answer.

This form of cushioning takes on an even more evident political function in example 8. By reversing the order of the apparently trivial words "always" and "not," the translation conveys the message that in some cases the wealth of a particular person or the poverty of another is indeed an evident expression of God's justice, whereas Calvin is clearly asserting the opposite.

Example 8

. . . *toujours nous ne verrons point . . . pourquoi Dieu aura enrichi l'un et qu'il aura laissé l'autre en sa pauvreté* (AB, 315)

We shall not always see for ourselves why God has enriched one person and left the other in poverty. (C. W. Bingham 1852)

We shall always not see . . . (ABE, 277)

On the other hand, Calvin certainly insists on the fallen nature of humans, who can be saved only by his grace freely given. Yet the translators manage to make that condition even more burdensome than Calvin himself. In example 9, the translator turns a comment about faulty understanding into one about morals.

Example 9

juger . . . à rebours, et prendre les choses en mauvaise part (AB, 311)

. . . wrongfully and wickedly (Anderson 1845)

. . . judging back to front and grasping [things] wrongly (ABE, 273)

The translators seem to be steeped in a culture where the nuclear family is taken for granted; that was not the culture which prevailed in the times and places where the Bible was written, nor does Calvin assume that it was, as can be seen in example 10.

Example 10

femmes et lignée (AB, 309)

wives and children (Anderson 1845)

wives and descendants (ABE, 272)

The same kind of bourgeois attitude appears in the individualism that translators introduce into the text even where Calvin explicitly states the opposite.

EXAMPLE 11
Après que tous eurent travaillé en commun . . . (AB, 336)
When they had all applied themselves . . . (C. W. Bingham 1852)
When they had all worked together . . . (ABE, 295)

A REFORMATION IS NOT A REVOLUTION

Just as Christianity grew away from Judaism, so the Reformation grew away from the Roman Catholic Church. It is standard in Reformed practice today to eschew the title "Saint" that the Catholic Church confers, but Calvin regularly used it. Translators such as Smail, Anderson, and Morrison omit it. That may be more comfortable for modern readers, but it is misleading with respect to Calvin in his own time.

TO SUM UP

Thus far I have used short extracts, which exposes my argument to the danger of quoting out of context. So let us consider an extensive passage. We shall find in it not only several of the biases that have already been pointed out but some further ones.

EXAMPLE 12
Prière pour le bon usage des biens matériels
Dieu tout puissant, puisque tu daignes bien t'abaisser jusques là, de prendre le soin et sollicitude pour nous entretenir de toutes choses qui sont nécessaires et expédientes pour passer par cette vie présente, fais que nous apprenions à nous reposer tellement sur toi, et nous assurer de ta bénédiction, que non seulement nous ne soyons adonnés ni à rapine ni autre maléfice, mais aussi que nous soyons éloignés de mauvaise convoitise, et que nous nous maintenions en ta sainte crainte; et par ce moyen nous apprenions aussi à endurer tellement pauvreté en ce monde, que prenant tout notre contentement et repos dans les richesses spirituelles, lesquelles tu nous offres par ton saint Évangile et desquelles tu nous fais dès à présent participants, nous tirions toujours allégrement à cette plénitude de tous biens, de laquelle nous jouirons lorsque nous serons parvenus à ce royaume céleste, et que nous serons en toute perfection conjoints et unis à toi, par Jésus-Christ notre Seigneur. Amen. (AB, 306)
Prayer for the proper use of material goods
Grant, Almighty God, that as thou deignest so far to condescend as to sustain the care of this life [2], and to supply us with whatever is needful for

our pilgrimage [3]—O grant that we may learn to rely on thee, and so to trust to thy blessing, as to abstain not only from all plunder and other evil deeds, but also from every unlawful [4] coveting; and to continue in thy fear, and so to learn also to bear our poverty on the earth [5], that being content with those spiritual riches which thou offerest to us in [6] thy gospel [7], and of which thou makest us now partakers [8], we may ever cheerfully aspire after that fullness of all blessings which we shall enjoin when at length we shall reach the celestial kingdom, and be perfectly united to thee, through Christ our Lord [9]. Amen. (Owen 1846)[4]

Almighty God, since you accept to stoop so far as to show the solicitude and take the care to supply us with whatever is needful and convenient for our journey through this present life, grant that we may learn to rely so fully on you, and so to trust to your blessing, as to abstain not only from all plunder and other evil deeds, but also from every wicked coveting, and to continue in your fear; and by these means to learn also so to bear our poverty on the earth that, finding our contentment and rest in those spiritual riches which you offer us through your holy gospel, and of which you make us partakers now already, we may ever cheerfully aspire after that fullness of all blessings which we shall enjoy when at length we shall reach the celestial kingdom and be perfectly united to you, through Jesus Christ our Lord. Amen. (ABE, 269)

Comments

1. Owen resorts to liturgical language that was archaic in 1846 when he was writing. Calvin wrote this prayer in the language of his day. The style chosen for this translation puts the prayer at a distance from the readers.
2. "Sustain the care of this life" is less practical or material than *nécessaires et expédients.* Calvin's phrase mentions separately not just what is necessary but what is simply convenient.
3. Calvin does not mention this Catholic concept. It contains notions both of the holiness of particular places and of the economic activity of the pilgrimage business, which sustained ecclesiastical institutions that Calvin considered parasitical.
4. Calvin is very careful not to confuse what is lawful with what conscience allows.
5. This passage, ended with a comma, is a call to resignation, whereas Calvin invites us to bear our poverty *in such a way* that we aspire to the blessings of the kingdom.
6. Owen refers to riches *in* the gospel, whereas Calvin is referring to the spiritual riches in the real world that are revealed *through* the gospels.
7. Owen omits the "holy."

4. The numbers in brackets in Owen's translation correspond to the "Comments" above.

8. "Thou makest us now partakers" is ambiguous. It could be understood as "henceforth we are offered the partaking in the hereafter"; Calvin is explicitly referring to the here and now (*dès à présent*).
9. Owen omits "Jesus."

A CLOSING WORD

As Calvin says, words "have their sauce" (ABE, 228). The flavor depends on the sauce as well as on the meat.

11

Translating Calvin into German

Peter Opitz

The purpose of this essay is to describe the problems one encounters when translating Calvin's Latin texts into German. This is a work I have been doing for several years in connection with the *Calvin Studienausgabe*, a selection of Calvin's important texts in modern German.

Instead of enumerating many items I will point out one single but crucial fact that is not limited to any specific modern language: Trying to translate Calvin is not only struggling with words and all the complex philosophical problems concerning the relationship between language and reality. It always means participating a little bit in transmitting the Gospel into a new culture as well.

One thing I have learned from this is that the more often Calvin uses certain words, and the more crucial they are to his texts, the harder they are to translate. The most important aid is, of course, the dictionary. But at the same time it is also the most dangerous, because it only contains words. The meaning of a word, however, only comes from its use in the language. This was stressed by language philosophers in the twentieth century, and rightly so. And this is true for all German terms that one finds in dictionaries when looking up Calvin's Latin words. Embedded in any language is a culture—in a sense, an entire understanding of the reality of the time when that language was, or is, actually used. Benjamin Whorf is correct here, even if he does sometimes exaggerate a bit.[1] That is also why computer-translated texts are fun to read but are not really useful (and often do not make much sense).

All cows in Switzerland look alike to people from the city, which is why they are simply called "cows." But they look very different from the farmer's perspective. They all have different names, depending on age, gender, or function. Farming would be impossible without this differentiation. And depending on whether one is a farmer, butcher, hiker, vegetarian, or bullfighter, whether one likes to eat ice cream, or whether one lives next to a cowshed, one also connects different expectations, hopes, or fears with the word "cow."

So what happens then, if instead of "cow" we talk about *doctrina* and *religio*? These two terms occur at important places in Calvin's works: His primary work is titled *Institutio christianae religionis*; it is instruction in the Christian *religio*. And when Calvin comes to the point that actually concerns him, he often speaks of the Christian *doctrina*.

Using these two words as examples, I would like to explain some problems in translating that cannot be solved with a dictionary. Of course, this can only be done here as a rough sketch.[2]

DOCTRINA

Cultural Connotations of *Doctrina*

The term *doctrina* comes up often in Calvin. If one looks in a dictionary for a German word for this term, one will first come across the German word *Lehre* ("teaching, doctrine, theory"). The *doctrina christiana* is the *christliche Lehre* ("Christian teaching/doctrine"). And with Calvin, often the translation of the term *doctrina* actually seems to make the most sense with *Lehre*.

However, if one calls to mind everything that is connected today—inside and outside the church—with the expression *Lehre*, then things will not seem so clear anymore. Since the Enlightenment, Christianity has been considered

1. See B. L. Whorf, *Language, Thought, and Reality* (Cambridge, MA: MIT Press, 1956).

2. My remarks concerning the term *doctrina* are based on my research on Calvin's hermeneutics published in Peter Opitz, *Calvins theologische Hermeneutik* (Neukirchen-Vluyn: Neukirchener Verlag, 1994). My comments about the term *religio* are developed further in Peter Opitz, "Calvins Gebrauch des Begriffs 'Religio,'" in *Calvin, Champion of the Gospel: Papers from the International Congress on Calvin Research, Seoul, 1998*, ed. David F. Wright, Antony N. S. Lane, Jon Balserak (Grand Rapids: Calvin Studies Society, 2006), 161–74.

more of a practical religion rather than a system of dogmas and firm doctrines one has to believe. With the expression *Lehre*, one connects a truth, formulated in clauses, and placed in front of us as strange phrases. *Lehren* are strange (and unfamiliar); they are authoritarian and have nothing to do with real life. Forced belief (or religious coercion) is carried out by means of *Lehren*. Yet religious conviction (or conviction of faith), it is said, is always subjective and personal. Expressions where the Latin root *doctrina* explicitly occurs in German confirm this: words such as *doktrinär* ("doctrinaire") or *Indoktrination* ("indoctrination") always have to do with influencing the opinions of other people by force.

Rigid *Lehren* are what must be combated. Whoever maintains the truth of certain *Lehren* will be suspected of being a fundamentalist. And the distance is not far from a fundamentalist to a person who through his or her *Lehre* becomes inhumane. This is the message that the media hammer into our heads day by day, and we Western Europeans grow up with this. Many people begin their theology studies with this conviction.

Calvin's Understanding of *Doctrina*

Calvin often uses—and in important places—the term *doctrina*. By this expression nothing else is meant at first than the "word of God." "Word of God" and *caelestis doctrina* are interchangeable expressions. The *doctrina* is *verbi sui doctrina* ("the doctrine/teaching of his word").[3] God shows himself through his word and lights the way toward us with the *doctrina*.[4] Accordingly, it can be said that the faith is in a permanent connection with the "word" or with *doctrina*.[5]

But the two expressions point in different directions in their meaning. While the term "word of God" has God as the subject—that is, it points to the origin of the "word," the term *doctrina* especially refers to the content and the arrival of the word of God on earth. The *doctrina* is the shape in which the word of God meets humankind.[6]

When Calvin prefers the term *doctrina*, he shows that he understands the word of God totally in its function of mediation between God and man. Of

3. *Calvini opera selecta*, 5 vols., ed. P. Barth and W. Niesel (Munich: Kaiser Verlag, 1926–1936), 3:264.2 (*Inst.* 2.2.21); hereafter *OS*. Compare with *doctrina*: E. Doumergue, *Jean Calvin, Tome IV* (1899), reprint Geneva 1969, 23f.

4. *OS* 5.9.32–33 (*Inst.* 4.1.5).

5. *OS* 4.14.8; 13.20 (*Inst.* 3.2.6).

6. "So that the true worship of God is placed before us, the beginning must be made with the heavenly doctrine/teaching (*caelestis doctrina*)" (*OS* 3.63.6–7 [*Inst.* 1.6.2]).

course, for Calvin a content is conveyed in the gospel. Something is said and, therefore, there is something for people to recognize and learn. But actually it concerns much more than just information on a subject taught by humans. The Christian *doctrina* receives its authority and power, after all, only from God himself.[7] This *doctrina* is an address, directed to human hearts in order to produce faith. True faith is not only knowledge but is an understanding that will be guided by the very "living God and his Christ" themselves.

The word of God is a word that teaches humans and at the same time concerns them; it includes them in the story of God. This is what the term *doctrina* is aiming at.

Calvin takes the term from the humanistic rhetorical tradition. As a rhetorical expression, *doctrina* points to the process of *docere*, that is, "in an appropriate and auditory way to present facts oratorically."[8] At the same time, the term *doctrina* possesses a pedagogical meaning. According to the humanistic understanding of education, the *doctrina* educates and forms the whole person.[9] *Docere* is *erudire*, as the humanistic scholar was "educated" in his whole human nature (*humanitas*)—also ethical and religious—through the study of the classical writers. Calvin's usage of the term *doctrina* shows that he is taking up the rhetorical as well as the pedagogical understanding of *doctrina*, and he interprets both of them theologically. He designates by this the movement of God through the word toward humankind, God showing himself in the word, and the reception of humankind by the word into the community of God.

Translation

With this, it is clear that the German term *Lehre* is not enough in this case and can even be misleading. It would be better to translate *doctrina* by the word *Verkündigung* ("preaching/heralding"), because it has in German both a content aspect and a performative one. It can describe the action and also the content. At the same time, it says that it concerns a dynamic action—not a rigid, inflexible truth, but a form of address. This translation does lose, however, the fact that *doctrina* with Calvin is not entirely covered by the sermon on Sunday morning, but has a dimension independent of being preached. There is no totally satisfactory German translation for *doctrina*.

7. "But our doctrine/teaching is raised above every worldly honour, above every might, and has to stay undefeated, because it is not ours, but the one of the living God and his Christ" (*OS* 3.12.9–11).

8. Cf. Cicero, *Orator ad M. Brutum* 32.113–33.118.

9. Cf. E. Kessler, *Das Problem des frühen Humanismus* [The Problem with Early Humanism] (Munich: Fink, 1968), 47–56.

RELIGIO

Cultural Connotations of *Religio*

Now I will try to give a rough outline of what is commonly understood in Western Europe by the term "religion." "Religion" is on the one hand a phenomenon of culture that can be observed. We talk about Christianity and Islam as world religions. An introduction to a religion consists, then, of an overview of its history, the story of how it spread, and its customs, traditions, practices, and concepts. With that we are practicing phenomenology: we are looking from the outside at a phenomenon that is foreign to us.

In connection with real people, we say that they are *religiös* ("religious"). We assume with this that religion is something subjective. It has its origin in *Gefühl* ("feelings, emotions") of the religious person. In that, every conceptualization is secondary and not actually important. There are many religions, since there are so many conceptualizations of this one unexplainable subjective. But these very conceptualizations are dangerous as well, because they also make claims of truth for others and then tend toward a know-it-all attitude and violence. It is better to cultivate a religiosity that concentrates on the individual and unexplainable than to talk about a god in a certain way. It is not done to talk about God, especially by people in public office. It is not only people outside the church who say that, but many people in the Christian church say it too. Thus, courses for pastors focus upon the care of individual religiosity (or religiousness) and the maintenance of spiritual experience. The contents thereof are less important. The main problem in our enlightened (and well-informed) culture is not which God is the true one, but whether religion can still have a place in this world that has lost its magic.

Calvin's Use of the Term

When Calvin uses the expression *religio*, he wants to do everything but defend religion. With this word he falls back on a very familiar Latin (not biblical) term that has a long pre-Christian and Christian tradition (Cicero, Seneca, Lactantius, Augustine). With Cicero the term *religio* describes the human reverence (*metus*) owed to God or the gods, which is manifested in certain religious actions (*cultus*) and is a public affair. This same understanding can also be found with Calvin. At the same time, Calvin can shift this term very close to *pietas*, at least when he is speaking about the true *religio*. But for Calvin, the distinction between *vera* and *falsa religio* is decisive—between true and false faith, between true and false worship of God—and this in view of an individual and his or her "inner self" as well as in view of the external presence of the church and also the state. Religion can never be a private matter. And one can only talk sensibly about religion if one at the same time asks for the truth.

Calvin does not create an anthropological theory about the religiosity of man. For him, it is not a matter of trying to prove that man is "religious" by nature. This phenomenon is undisputed, even by the Epicureans.[10] His way is not from the general to the particular, from religion in general to Christianity specifically. His approach is exactly the reverse: God's revelation in his word makes human relationship with God accessible, influenced by the dialectic of the matter of creation and sinfulness. The activity of human *religio* is for Calvin always the wrong *religio*; it is superstition, because the human heart is a factory of idols.

Translation

How should one then translate the title of Calvin's *Institutio* into German? Otto Weber, in his German translation that is still definitive, does not substitute for the term religion: *Unterricht in der christlichen Religion* ("Instruction/Lesson in Christian Religion"). Given the different connotations of "religion" in sixteenth-century Geneva and twenty-first-century Germany, is this rendition what one calls in translator circles a "false friend"?

One could translate *religio* with *Glaube* (faith), as Spiess did in his otherwise poor 1536 translation of *Institutio.* He retitled Calvin's work *Christliche Glaubenslehre* ("Christian Dogma/Teaching of Faith"). He thus maintained some of what Calvin wants to say, but he also lost some. Calvin is not only concerned about the individual aspect but also about the shaping of the "true faith" in the church. According to Calvin, to a right (kind of) church belongs—as everybody knows—also the right (kind of) order. Besides this, the term *Glaube* runs the risk of being understood in the Lutheran form of law and gospel. For Calvin, this would be too restricted. According to Calvin, the shaping of human life, the *Ethik* according to the Decalogue, definitely belongs to *vera religio.* In the French preface to the *Institutio* of 1560, Calvin speaks about the *philosophie Chrestienne* ("Christian philosophy," *OS* 3.7.31–32) and means by this an extensive teaching of life, as distinguished from speculative scholastic questions.

A third possibility would be to interpret *religio* in the title of *Institutio* by *Gottesverehrung* ("worship of God"/"worshiping God"). With that, one would have met an important intention of Calvin yet at the same time provoked the misunderstanding that *Institutio* concentrates on liturgical questions.

Here too there seems to be no solution that would be totally satisfactory. Probably there is no other way than to use different words for *religio*, to say

10. *Extra controversiam* (*Inst.* 2.3.1 = *OS* 3.37.17).

things differently depending on the context, and to hope that those studying the *Institutio* will read it themselves and thus better learn themselves what Calvin meant.

CONCLUSION

In short, with Calvin's handling of expressions one rediscovers that the meaning of a word is only shown from its use in the language. Consequently, in order to let Calvin speak to us today, we have as a first step to be aware of the cultural context in which he used his words and of the difference between his time and ours, because it is possible to use his words and say other things than he did. But it is also possible to use other words than he did and say very similar things to those he wanted to say. Translating is a tricky thing. To be aware of this fact does not lead to resignation. Instead, it can help us support the always surprising capacity of human language to connect cultures and to make real translations possible.

Contributors

James D. Bratt, Professor of History, Calvin College, Grand Rapids, Michigan

Eberhard Busch, Emeritus Professor of Reformed Theology, University of Göttingen

François Dermange, Professor of Ethics, Faculty of Theology, University of Geneva

Edward Dommen, President of the Scientific Committee, Geneva International Academic Network, and Economist Emeritus, United Nations Conference on Trade and Development (UNCTAD)

Eduardo Galasso Faria, Professor of Theology, Seminário Teológico de São Paulo, São Paulo, Brazil

Robert M. Kingdon, Emeritus Professor of History, University of Wisconsin-Madison

Elsie Anne McKee, Professor of Reformation Studies and the History of Worship, Princeton Theological Seminary

Peter Opitz, Privatdozent for Church History, and Oberassistent at the Institute for the History of the Swiss Reformation at the University of Zurich.

Seong-Won Park, Professor of Theology, Young Nam Theological College and Seminary, Korea

Christoph Stückelberger, Professor of Ethics, Theological Faculty, University of Basel, and Director, Institute of Theology and Ethics of the Federation of Swiss Protestant Churches, Bern, Switzerland

Index